GOOD COMMANDER,
BAD COMMANDER

RICK HANCOCK

ISBN 978-1-0980-2980-7 (paperback)
ISBN 978-1-0980-2981-4 (digital)

Christian Faith Publishing, Inc.
832 Park Avenue
Meadville, PA 16335
www.christianfaithpublishing.com

Printed in the United States of America

INTRODUCTION

If you never have trouble with your boss, don't bother reading this. If you never wonder, "What is God doing with me?" don't bother reading this. The short stories I will tell are all true and are my personal experiences while in the Army. The reason I tell them is that it's my hope that they are an encouragement to anyone who faces similar problems in their jobs and to reassure you that God is watching over you and has a plan for you. You do the right thing every time and let God handle the fall out. Again, if you never have these problems and questions, you should put this aside and read something else.

CHAPTER 1

Writing Is Hard

*"Sometimes it's interesting to see
just how bad, bad writing can be."*
—Joe Gillis,
Sunset Boulevard

I'm only a "C" student. School has always been difficult for me. When you are young what exactly is school anyway? For me and my seven brothers and sisters, and later my three additional stepbrothers, school was simply the place where they warehoused us during the daytime. The little town I grew up in had six neighborhood elementary schools and through no misconduct on my part, I attended five of them. The school where I spent half of fourth grade had a hot lunch program and for that year it was the one good meal we would get during the day. We all still remember that as a good school. School's secondary purpose was to give my poor mother a break from her two alternating tasks of either entertaining us or breaking up our fights, which would erupt over the most petty and stupid of reasons.

In my family, academic achievement was defined by my mother who gave us two clear requirements. The first one was the near term or daily challenge which was "don't you dare get put on probation, I'm not raising a bunch of losers" my mother would say. "And I'm not kidding" was her best way of putting punctuation on it. But the second and ultimate strategic goal was that we that we had to graduate from high school. That threat was one of my earliest memories regarding school, "If you drop out of school you can't live here anymore, I'm not raising a house full of losers" my mother would tell us. I suppose she said this whenever she sensed that we needed some academic motivation or saw one of the neighbors with another young adult loafing and freeloading off their parents. "What a bunch of losers," she would say.

Now that I'm old, I'm ashamed of myself that I didn't reach down and help my younger brothers and sisters get their arms around school. Instead we all simply tried to get through every day on our own. Not being smart, my own daily problems were enough to occupy my mind. Like the time in sixth grade when my mother spanked me for crying because I didn't want to wear my older sister's pants to school. "Be glad you have those pants to wear, some kids don't have pants and it's ten degrees below zero," she told me. I knew how cold it was because we left the water running in the sink overnight so it wouldn't freeze. But when it's that cold it froze anyway and each faucet produced ice cycles running into the sink. And regardless of the cold, by sixth grade even the most socially challenged child is conscious of social norms and a boy wearing girls pants can expect the other kids to tease him. The only question was whether I was going to get in a fight over it.

I think school was hardest in the wintertime. It seemed like our feet were always wet and cold. If it was warm outside, the slush made your feet wet. If it was cold outside the snow melted when you entered a building and made your feet wet. Either way you were wet and a boy wearing his sister's pants doesn't have an extra set of dry cloths to change into. But the worse thing about winter was the school class Christmas parties. The poor teachers were trying to do something nice so we would have an afternoon when the class would have a Christmas party with gift exchange. There would be a drawing of names and you were required to bring a gift for the person whose name you drew. There would be some small limit on the price of the gift in the attempt to keep things under control and not to put stress on the poor families like mine. So my mother did her best to provide gifts for kids she didn't know at a time when she didn't have money for gifts for her own children. Inevitably these gifts were pretty lousy gifts.

This became evident in fifth grade when the lucky girl who received her gift from me gave it back and asked for the one I had received. Of course I was happy to make this exchange. I guess that was a particularly bleak year because that night my mother was upset that four of us came home with the gifts we had taken with us that morning. "What are you kids thinking? Who comes home with the presents you were supposed to give away, what can you possibly be thinking?" she asked. We all know that these were simply lousy gifts but how do you explain that to your mother without hurting her feelings? Well you can't explain it so we didn't try, we all kept it a secret among ourselves and chaffed at the humiliation of it.

The next year, I conspired to avoid a repeat of this disaster by pretending I was sick that day and told my mother that I wasn't going to school. But my mother would have none if it and attacked with one of her standard threats, "If you don't go to school I'm not writing you an excuse note and you know what that means, it means probation for skipping school." That was always the end of the discussion and watching me crash and burn was a warning to everyone else to put on their coats and get out of the house before things got ugly. I think that year marked a point where I began retreating from social events at school. I remember thinking, this poor teacher, Mrs. Riddle, she thinks she is doing such a nice thing but this is really killing me. I still avoid Christmas parties.

Beside the lack of any understanding about the purpose of school, my life as a "C student" was supported by the fact that I was and still am, a really poor reader. Most of my friends were poor readers so

I didn't identify how this feed failure into other subjects and most importantly failure in writing. Writing is after all, the point of this chapter. I didn't master the mechanics of language starting with spelling, construction of sentences, and all the rules of grammar. You know what I mean: "*i* before e except after *c*" and "when two vowels go walking the first one does the talking," and all that crap. So when it came to writing a dreaded book report or an insurmountable theme paper I was totally unequipped. For years I would get the standard "C-" with no comments on what I had written beyond the comments of "bad spelling" and "poor grammar" which I learned to expect. Since I didn't understand these foundational things the whole world of writing was placed in the category of things I knew I simply can't do (brain surgery, no; four-minute mile, no; writing, no).

I had a temporary writing breakthrough my senior year of high school in Mr. Phiffer's English Class. I had desperately tried to avoid attending my senior year but a couple of things conspired to keep me in school. Although I was still living under the prime directive of "if you drop out of school you can't live here anymore, I'm not raising a house full of losers," I proposed an alternative that my mother and new stepfather both embraced. That summer I had a job washing dishes in a seasonal restaurant being paid the federally mandated new minimum wage of $1.25 hour. I'm not a student of social policy so I don't know if the government intends for a man to support a family on minimum wage but I can say that it is a life saver when you are the bottom of the food chain. My proposal to my parents was that I would get a full time job during the day and finish the remaining high school requirements at night. The end result would be that I would graduate on schedule while working the entire year. "Brilliant, see the benefit of your eleven years of school" my parents agreed.

My mother agreed to write an absentee note for school and the next day I skipped school and looked for a job. I lived in a small town on Lake Superior and I could walk to all the businesses that remained open during what was called the "off season." The "off season" were the months Oct through May when it snowed and tourists didn't come in enough numbers to support much of an economy. We always joked that summer was only three months of bad sledding.

The unemployment rate for adult men in my county was 50 percent. People everywhere know about Appalachia but we had a lower per capita income then they did. So in this economically depressed area I started looking for a full time day job. The first placed I approached was Barish Brothers Clothing Store. The lady was nice and when she took my application she asked "How old are you?"

"Sixteen," I replied, "and I will be seventeen in November."

"I'm sorry," she said. "We only hire sixteen-year-olds in the summer, you must be eighteen to work in the winter." My next target was JC Penny's where they had a very attractive position as the stock boy.

Before giving me the application the manger asked me, "How old are you?"

"Eighteen, sir" was my immediate reply.

"Okay," he said, "You can fill out an application but we have twenty people on the waiting list to be the stock boy and some are guys who just returned from Vietnam so your chances are slim."

So I spent that day lying about my age to anyone who would possible give me a job. As I walked between the businesses, I thought of different ways I would avoid questions about proving my age like "my driver's license is at home, I'll bring it back when you hire me." But no one asked me to prove my age because they knew they weren't going to hire me anyway. That night I reported in at home and we were all disappointed that I didn't find a job and I would stay in regular day time high school.

Enter Mr. Phiffer. Since I was staying in school, I had to pick my classes. The wrestling coach thought he could get me into the local state college, which was starting a wrestling program. No one from my family or friends had ever gone to college so this was not really an objective for me but on the outside chance that I did attempt college, taking Senior English would be a good thing to do. Senior English was 100 percent about writing and my probability of success was extremely low but even if I flunked I would still graduate.

On the first writing assignment I received an "A" with no comments about spelling, etc. Yes, I got an "A"! I remained after class and spoke with Mr. Phiffer and told him how surprised I was because I never had success at English classes. His response was the most amazing thing "I know what all of your grades have been—but that isn't what my class is about, you can think clearly and you can communicate your thoughts; that is what this class is about." For the first time ever, I have a favorite teacher. And he's a damn English Teacher! He's not even the coach of the football, cross country, wrestling, track or hockey (hockey continues to be my all-time favorite sport) teams. And it was also remarkable that he had looked at my school records, this had never occurred to me. What kind of teacher does that?

When we got our first report card I had an "A" in Senior English. The only one more surprised than me was Ms. Falls who was my Homeroom teacher. Ms. Falls had also been my eleventh-grade American Literature teacher so she knew that I had been unable to appreciate Poe and Hawthorne. You know that "bells, bells, bells" malarkey. I'm absolutely certain that those guys never played hockey. It was in homeroom where your report card was given to you to take home, get signed by your parents acknowledging they have seen your scores and returned for the cycle to repeat. At that period of my life the report card was not something I took pride in. My friend "Chewy" was a good student and used to have his high school report cards framed in his bedroom but I think his second wife made him take them down. Poor Chewy. Ms. Falls kept me after Homeroom Session that day and asked me how I could get an A in Senior English.

I told her what Mr. Phiffer had told me. She thought for a moment and said, "Yes, you do think well, but spelling and grammar are also important."

Later it occurred to me that she might have suspected that I had found a way to cheat and how splendid it would have been if she had approached Mr. Phiffer with her suspicion. "No," Mr. Phiffer would respond, "he just thinks and communicates well."

"Unbelievable," I'm sure she would respond.

My year in Senior English was so enjoyable. Who knew school could be like this? I experimented with a couple of things with varying success. One time I got real creative (creative for a wrestler/hockey player). Sue Drow and Cathy Dahl really liked it but Mr. Phiffer said no, despite what I was trying to do it wasn't the assignment. But no harm no foul, good try but just stick to the assignment.

The thing that made high school bearable was the high school sports programs. I was not a gifted athlete, but I enjoyed sports tremendously and they ensured that I had little free time to get into trouble. My stepbrothers and most of my friends thought I was foolish to give up my free time and my submission to the rigor of daily practice. Many of them drifted into delinquency and alcohol but sports always gave me an excuse to be unavailable and not get involved in those activities. My daughters have asked me how one of the poorest kids in school could participate in sports programs. The answer is simple, they were free. It sounds remarkable today but there were no "activity fees" for high school sponsored programs and even the amateur hockey program (one of the best in the country) was free due to sponsors and fund raising. I just had to commit my time and effort.

Remarkably the next year, largely under the direction of the wrestling coach, I enrolled at the local college. I believe that God has a plan for each of us. That plan isn't necessarily what we want or think it should be but God opens and closes doors. One year prior I not only had no intention of going to college but I was trying to get a job as a stock boy to get out of high school. Now I'm in college. So, one door closed and another one opened for me. It also shows me what a mess I can make of things if I rely only on my own intelligence.

In college, I had mixed results with English Classes and writing papers. My first English professor had a zero tolerance for spelling errors. "If you can't spell, you don't belong here," he told me. If I was doing an assignment out of class I could take the time to look up the correct spelling but when it was an assignment to write a paper during the nine-ty-minute class, I was in a deep hole so I only used words that I had memorized. Over the years, I have memorized a lot of misspelled words (is it helicopter or helicoptor?). This professor also told me that my writing style was unacceptable because it was "too conversational." So I struggled to develop a more "direct style" and I was once again a struggling "C student." But largely I found that each professor had a preferred style and if I did it his/her way then I could minimally get through. But I'm not an intuitive person who could quickly size up the instructor and know what he wants. My friend Chewy could do this. No, I had a pattern where I would try hard and fail and then struggle to recover. End result for college was final GPA of 2.5 on a 4-point scale. A solid "C." Yes, it was a miracle.

Another door that God opened for me was Army ROTC. This was the early 1970s and the Army was so unpopular that they could not fill their classes at West Point and colleges were dropping ROTC programs. For me the Army was a wonderful opportunity but I won't bore you with that here. To be commissioned a second lieutenant you had to complete the ROTC requirements and graduate on time with a C average. The cadets with good grades were commissioned as Engineers, Finance and Military Intelligence types. I wanted to be an Infantry Paratrooper and to do that the only requirement beyond graduation was that you be able to run five miles and then throw a grenade into a third floor window. Thanks to high school athletics, I could meet this five-mile/grenade requirement in combat boots, on snow shoes and while legally drunk so I was essentially a triple threat.

During my time in the Army, I learned a very direct writing approach which the Army called "Effective Writing." The instructions to program your VCR fall into this category. My wife once asked me, "How do you write like this?" I guess it is the "Dragnet Style" of writing. If you remember the old TV series where Detective Friday would correct someone giving a statement with the remark "just the facts mame, just tell me the facts." I've also been told that it is the style of writing best suited to high performing Asperger's people. You can't write a speech like this but it is good for a wide range of technical writing like operations orders and contracts. I had some success at this and as an Army captain actually wrote two articles on Army helicopter tactics that were published in an official Department of Defense Magazine.

But the real essence of writing still alluded me and when I was a student at the US Army Command and General Staff College at Ft. Leavenworth Kansas, I flunked writing again. This is a charm school for majors whom the Army believes have the potential to become senior officers. The writing examination consists of a ninety-minute session in the classroom where you write an "argumentative paper" on the subject the instructor picks out of his head and writes on the chalk board. In the Army style, the argumentative paper has three parts—introduction, body, conclusion, and each of them have three or four discrete elements. The instructor then grades the papers and selects twenty students for remedial writing instruction. Not nineteen, not twenty-one but the quota is twenty students to fill the Remedial Writing Class. In the Army, it's important to hit your performance standards so that no one can challenge your judgments. If the requirement is twenty, and I give you something different then I can expect to explain why I did this. The instructor can't say something like "I have a PHD in literature and believe that only three students are deficient." If he did this he could expect to be reprimanded with "no, are you nuts, you can't make judgments that way, you give me a list of twenty, who do you think you are anyway?" After receiving my failing grade I sat down with the Chief of the "Effective Writing Department" and walked through the mechanics of my paper and asked what was wrong.

He said, "There is nothing wrong with your paper, structure, spelling, grammar are all okay, it simply doesn't ring my bell, it's dry, maybe it should be more conversational. But this isn't a big deal, you will be a better writer after Remedial Writing." I told him, "But I don't understand what that standard is or how I can meet it." He responded in classic Army fashion, "Look, major, I have to pick twenty people for Remedial Writing, and I'm not changing my list. I'm a colonel and you're a major so you can leave my office now." So that was that, I put on my coat and left before things got ugly. At this school Remedial Writing Class is referred to as "Bonehead English" and no one wants to be identified as attending this class.

But I had learned in elementary school that it is best to face humiliation without flinching. Someone would ask me, "Rick, what class do you have this afternoon?"

"Bonehead English," I would respond doing my best to show no weakness or feeling of shame. "I'm sorry, I hope this all works out for you" would be a good reply. Yes, this is what a leper feels like. There were maybe three guys in the class that really did have trouble writing and I formed a support group to compare notes and encourage each other. Funny to think of it now but there were no females in the class.

I did just fine in Bonehead and sort of as an act of rebellion I wrote and published two more Articles the next year. When I wrote these new Articles I had the lyrics of the old Lesly Gore song "You Don't Own Me" playing in my head.

But in the Army, they do own you and about a month before graduation I was called into the office of a different colonel and told that I had been on academic probation for the last three months because I had flunked the writing exam. My first thought was "You rat bastards, you cowards, if you had told me this when you flunked me I wouldn't have simply left your office without doing my best to ring your bell." My second thought was "I can't let my mother know that I'm on probation because I know she will think I'm a loser." If I'm lucky, she might say something like "I'm sorry, I hope this all works out for you." My mother died twenty-five years later and I hope she never learned about this failure.

After the Command and General Staff College I was assigned into the Army Acquisition Corp where I would write contracts and program management documentation. I had good success at doing this and some of my documents like the "Risk Management Plan for the Comanche Helicopter Program" were used as instructional material at the Defense Systems

Management College. Other documents were used in the government's litigation proceedings before the Armed Service Board of Contract Appeals. Since leaving the Army I have been able to make a comfortable living doing this same type of work, which is essentially writing stuff for senior managers who can't write themselves. This is not glamorous work and one of my friends describes it as "following the elephants in the parade and cleaning up their messes."

I don't write well, but I love to tell stories about my Army experiences. I most often tell them because they are useful in encouraging people who have a problem. An example is the men's prayer groups at church when someone reveals that they have a problem which is similar to an experience I had in the Army. For example, your boss tells you to do something illegal which you refuse to do and as a consequence you find yourself unemployed in a way that isn't directly traceable to your rejection of your boss' instruction. Yes, I know you're surprised but this happens in the Army every day. People are surprised when I reveal that I've been fired from jobs. "What, you've been fired?" they will ask in bewilderment.

I always answer truthfully, "Yes, maybe six times over the last forty years. The first time I was an Army captain and I got fired by a general. It broke my heart and I thought it was the end of my career but within six months I knew it was the best thing that could have happened to me. That first firing gave me the correct perspective to avoid similar problems and to prepare me for the firings that happened later."

For the last five years, I've attended a prayer group on Tuesday morning before everyone goes to work. A few weeks ago, my friend Dave, who works in sales for an international appliance company, told us that a major account was taken away from him at the request of that customer. He said it really hurt his feelings and that he was processing this in the same manner as if he had been fired. "Then I thought about you getting fired six times and I suddenly had to laugh and realize that my situation wasn't unique," he told me.

"I'm glad my failures can provide you comic relief—someday I will tell you about all the times I flunked English," I told him.

Through the course of telling these stories I have been encouraged to write this book. Since I have actually read very few books, I'm clueless about how to write a book so I applied what I have been doing for years and came up with a solid "effective writing" approach. I wrote a draft and asked a few friends who had encouraged me to write this in the first place to give some unfiltered feedback. If you ever do this you have to be really careful about who you ask to review your work. Someone described it as test of friendship and you have to be careful for two very practical reasons.

First, some people will want to take over the project and are offended if you don't accept every idea they give you or if you try to retain ownership. These people act as if it is their damn book. Second, some people don't want the responsibility of providing "critical" feedback. They are reluctant because they love you and they know this can get messy. I floated my draft by three carefully selected people.

The first person I gave it to was Ed Daigle, a friend from church who was the first person to encouraged me to write the book. I think Christians in general can be expected to give critical feedback. Ed was also a good choice because he had no military experience and his feedback was "I don't know what the Armed Services Board of Contract Appeals is or why it's important. When you tell a story it's interesting, but when you write it this way it's not. My assessment is that people in the Army might read it but I'm not sure that anyone will read it if they aren't already your friend. You also need to add stories that explain what type of person you are. What makes you happy, what makes you sad, that sort of stuff."

"This makes me feel like an insurance salesman and our church membership is getting smaller," I observed.

The second person I gave it to was Brian Lareau, one of my employees in Detroit. Brian had several years as an Army Officer and he is in no way intimidated by me. His feedback was "I see how this all comes together and it's interesting how you explained the Officer Evaluation and Promotion System, especially the PowerPoint slide. But I'm not sure that anyone who is not one of your employees will read it."

"Ouch! And I don't have as many employees as I did three years ago," I thought.

The third person was the most enthusiastic but also gave me the most concern. The third person was my daughter Theresa and the concern was that she would be afraid of hurting my feelings. Like I didn't want to hurt my mother in fifth grade over lousy Christmas presents at school, Theresa wouldn't want to hurt my feelings over my lousy writing. Nonetheless, I asked her to give me some unfiltered feedback. Theresa is a singularly good choice to be a writing coach for anybody. She was the valedictorian at Providence College, has a master's degree from Brown University, and is always the best writer in school and at work. She reviewed my draft plus the comments from Ed and Brian and she tactfully said, "I agree with both of them, I think the style is too technical". I told her "I just can't brake free of the Army Effective Writing Style" so she gave me some examples of authors who write in a conversational style and some very practical guidance.

So the verdict was clear that I had to write this book in a conversational style. A big part of that change is shifting from telling the facts of a story to discussing how I feel about those facts. This bothers me tremendously. Talking to a couple of people about getting fired and having my feelings hurt is okay, but I don't like exposing myself like that to strangers. When I told Ed about my reservations about being open he told me, "You're an old man, what do you care what strangers think of you?" Another problem is how to organize the material. Doing it chronologically seems to be the only logical way to do it, but I'm thinking like an Army guy when I say this. Where to place a statement about the purpose of the book also had to be rethought. My training is that this has to be the first thing you write (bottom line upfront— BLUF) but it seems to make sense to put it here at the end of chapter 1 and not the beginning. What words are capitalized is another major difference. Oh man, when worlds collide, it is so unnerving. In fact, this whole chapter is new and a result of the advice I received. If you think it's dribble, you're probably right.

So let me give a clear statement for the purpose of this book. The short stories I will tell are all true and are my personal experiences with bad leaders in the Army. They all describe normal human behaviors that are common in both military and civilian leaders and we all suffer under bad or incompetent managers at some time. What people find interesting is that in the Army culture these behaviors are amped up on steroids because of the power structure and the ability of senior leaders to act totally arbitrarily with little fear of being held accountable for their bad behavior. The reason I tell them is that it's my hope that they are an encouragement to anyone who faces similar problems in their jobs and to reassure you that God is watching over you and has a plan for you. You do the right thing every time and let God handle the fall out. If you don't ever have problems with your managers, you should put this aside and read something else.

CHAPTER 2

I'm Too Smart to Be an Infantryman

My initial assignment after Infantry Officer Basic was thirteen months in Korea. At the replacement unit in Seoul, someone in the back room drew the wrong straw for me and I was diverted from the Second Infantry Division on the DMZ to an Infantry Security Company at an Ammunition Ordnance Depot in an isolated location to the south. The Infantry company provided perimeter security for a Depot that stored weapons. We are told "there are no bad jobs in the Army" and this is somewhat, pretty much, almost always true. But the fact is that some jobs are not in the mainstream of what you need for professional development and for a new Infantry second lieutenant this security company was well out of

24

the mainstream. Years later as a major at the Army Command and General Staff College, I was at a party at Major John Krysa's house and one of the generals present asked a group of about ten of us what our first assignments had been. Remarkably half said the Eighty-Second Airborne Division. I held back from saying anything until the general looked at me and asked, "What about you?"

"Security company at an Ordnance depot in Korea," I responded.

"How did you get here?" he asked in puzzlement. So yes, there are no bad jobs in the Army but clearly some jobs lead to longer careers.

So I was one of three Infantry officers in the Infantry security company in a depot that was commanded by an Ordnance Branch lieutenant colonel (LTC). My efficiency reports were scored by my Infantry branch captain company commander as my rater and the Ordnance Branch lieutenant colonel depot commander as my senior rater. This becomes important later in the story so I am doing what Theresa told me is "foreshadowing." The depot commander had many organizational problems and immediately assigned me the full time duty as the depot motor officer to run the motor pool with 250 vehicles. I did this for seven months and really enjoyed vehicle maintenance. I liked the soldiers who were the mechanics and their work ethic. I liked learning the maintenance and supply systems. I liked prioritizing work and allocating the resources I controlled. I learned about inventorying tools, which would benefit me many times in later assignments. There was the unfortunate misunderstanding when our higher headquarters conducted a small investigation when they learned about my unauthorized switching of the transfer cases between two dead-lined wreckers. By the regulations, I was supposed to send them both to higher level maintenance organization 180 miles away, but I would lose them both for a couple of months so I decided to do it in-house. To my relief, my transgression was attributed to my inexperience and enthusiasm and on the positive side I did produce one operational wrecker so the investigation was quietly dismissed.

Despite my mistakes, I found that I could discuss a number of things with the depot commander. After six months I met with the commander and asked what I should do when I left Korea. For example should I go to the Maintenance Officers Course, etc. He gave me the following advice: "You had the misfortune of being assigned here and not in the Infantry division where you would have learned basic Infantry skills—that is what you need to do—you need to go to a real Infantry maneuver unit and learn to control troops moving through the woods, control them during live fire, motivate them when they're tired/hungry/cold, etc., you will see if you are good it and if that is what you want to do as a career." What terrific advice!

"How exactly do I do that?" I asked him.

"You have to get out ahead of the officer who is deciding your next assignment and request that he send you somewhere that is predominantly filled with maneuver units. If you simply rotate back to the US, you might end up teaching marksmanship at Ft. Polk Louisiana which is after all, a legitimate assignment for an Infantry lieutenant. Your best chance of a maneuver unit is to request Germany where almost all positions are in maneuver units" he responded.

So I immediately wrote a letter to the Military Personnel Center (MILPERCEN) and asked that they not send me not back to the US but to send me to Germany instead. Happily there was a Christmas Miracle and I received orders to the US Army Berlin Brigade. You can't get any deeper into Germany then Berlin. The world map has changed since then but at that time Berlin was still under the WWII Occupation Agreement and was 110 miles beyond the iron curtain and was divided into the American, Soviet, French, and English sectors. My oldest daughter Theresa (yes, my writing coach) was born in the US Army Hospital in Berlin and has a birth certificate from all four of these countries. So I wasn't simply going to Germany, I was going 110 miles inside Soviet-controlled East Germany. Yes, for the 1970s "Peace Time, Cold War Army" this was going to be "Real Infantry."

This year in Korea was a tough year. I got married before going on active duty and Korea was what was called "an unaccompanied tour." This meant that you were not allowed to bring your spouse so my wife was waiting for me back home. None of us had our wives there so we didn't whine or sulk about it. This was also a really miserable time for the Army. On the global stage this was the year we left Vietnam and the evening news was full of Vietnamese pilots crashing their helicopters next to Navy ships in a frantic effort to escape. One of our new Air Force C-5 transports crashed enroute back to the US with several hundred Vietnamese orphans. It was like we couldn't get out of our own way and nothing could go right. Things were also miserable at our little Depot. Despite having a really great depot commander, I was working through problems I never expected to face. I cannot make these things up. The company commanders of the Ordnance and Military Police Companies (yes, Military Police) were absolutely ineffective and could not control their units. Race tensions were always on edge and we had a racial fight at least once a month but these commanders could not lay the law down and establish discipline. Drug use was rampant but again no actions by those commanders were taken. The MP soldiers were mostly white and the Ordnance soldiers were mostly black and both could get equally drunk and stupid and fights would start. There was a half dozen Ordnance officers who could not be given responsibilities so they were kind of like ghosts always around but they didn't have jobs. When they had post duty officer you might find them off post in a bar.

I didn't realize it at the time but the most significant and most fortunate aspect of this entire year was that the two other Infantry officers were black men. These were the first black men that I had ever known and the time I spent with them was pivotal in my development as an officer and as a man. Joe Omby was my company commander and Terry Franklin was the executive officer whom I later replaced. In the midst of what to me was racial chaos, these two men took the time to patiently explain the underlying racial problems that were being played out in America and at our depot. Joe gave me Eldridge Cleaver's book "Soul on Ice" and when I told him I didn't understand most of it, he patiently explain what Clever was trying to say. Terry had gone to Tuskegee University and was a terrific athlete and taught Joe and I how to play tennis. Sometime after Terry rotated back to the US, Joe and I won the Depot Tennis Doubles Championship. Joe left the Army after six years and became a lawyer in Houston. Some years later I needed to contact Joe so I called his mother in Bowling Green Kentucky and her first response was, "You're that Canadian guy that served with Joe in Korea, he always spoke so highly of you." Obviously I speak highly of Joe also.

It think that I should note that for people my age, the race problem I poorly described above seems like a faded memory and young people don't know what I'm talking about at all. I think a gage or marker might be the establishment of the Martin Luther King National Holiday. Although it's now just a day off in January and part of life, nationally it was a divisive and contentious issue. It was first proposed to congress in 1968, it was defeated in congress in 1979, not passed/signed into law until 1983 and the last state finally recognized it in 2000. Today we have a healthy national dialogue about race relations and fairness but it is completly different than the open daily racially problems in the 1970s America and the Army that I'm trying to describe.

As I said earlier, I ran the motor pool for seven months. When it was time to change jobs the depot commander had me in to discuss where he would put me. The obvious position was the executive officer in the Infantry company but he surprised me when he asked if I would consider taking over the Ammunition Platoon in the Ordnance company. He confided that although this was a position for an Ordnance captain, that he was hesitant to put any of his available captains into the job because they couldn't lead. He also knew that if he put me, an Infantry second lieutenant into the job, that I would be in a shit fight every day with enlisted men that wouldn't want to work for me and the disgruntled captains who would be mad that I took their job. Despite this gloomy outlook he assured me that his deliberations were not about me doing the job, he knew I was tough enough to do the job, but he wasn't sure it would be fair to me. Another factor was that he would be reassigned back to the states in three months and he had to consider how to best position the depot for his replacement. Of course, I was flattered beyond belief and told him I would do any job he wanted me to. Two weeks later, I replaced Terry Franklin as the executive officer in the Infantry company.

Three months later, the depot commander departed for his next stateside assignment. Within the first few weeks I was bewildered to watch a strange change in what I guessed was the power structure of the depot. First, the new commander went out of his way to openly discredit his predecessor. The second thing that happened was that the "ghost officers" who had proven to be unmotivated, ineffective, and unreliable were now in the new commanders inner circle as his trusted advisors. They were kind of like "Eddie Haskels" from the old "Leave it to Beaver Show," "Gee, Mrs. Cleaver, you are so much smarter than the other moms." I was bewildered by this, but I saw this repeated many times over the next nineteen years. As for me, I had orders to go to Germany so I was just watching the targets in my lane and not involved in the petty intrigues at depot headquarters.

Two weeks before my departure for Germany, the Infantry NCOs gave me a going-away party. This was the first such party (they had not done this for Terry) and I was flattered beyond belief. Of course the new depot commander was invited to attend. It would have been rude to not invite him. The NCOs gave me a nice going-away memento, which still hangs on my "I love me" wall, and I was asked to speak. I said that it had been a long difficult year and I was looking forward to going to Germany and being in a real Infantry maneuver unit. Most of what I said was parroting the things the previous depot commander had said to me. Applause, cheering, drinking, pushups, etc., and it was a great party.

The next Monday morning, the roof fell in on me when I was called to the depot commander's office. I remember that the sergeant major, who had been a good advisor to me, was acting funny and avoided making eye contact with me. The door to the commander's office opened and the Infantry second lieutenant replacing me came out. He was crying and rushed past me without acknowledging me. "What in the hell is this?" I wondered. A side note here is that this second lieutenant was from Clemson University. He is the only person I ever met from Clemson. I know I'm being petty but because of this crying episode, I always cheer against the Clemson Tiger teams and I'm disappointed when they win the National Football Championships.

As I entered the commander's office he called me to attention in front of his desk. He opened the conversation with "You insulted me in front of all those people when you said you are anxious and happy to go to a real Infantry unit." I had absolutely no idea why he was mad.

I responded, "Sir, It was certainly not my intention to insult you."

He quickly accelerated the attack by saying, "I was commissioned into the Infantry but after two years I realized I was too smart for the Infantry and changed to Ordnance. Only stupid people are in the Infantry." Okay, I thought, "This is why the new guy is crying but I'll be damned if he's going to bully me."

I responded politely, "I really don't know what to say about that."

He gave me more of his experience with Infantry guys by saying, "When I was in Vietnam as an Ordnance captain all the Infantry guys left with a sack of medals and I didn't get any." He's the depot commander and I'm a second lieutenant so I couldn't appear to be combative but I wasn't going to be a floor mat for this guy so I said, "I wasn't in Vietnam sir, but maybe that was because they were out in the bush engaged in combat." He used one of what I suspect to be his well-worn victim's speech and said, "No, it's because the combat arms (Infantry, Armor, Artillery) branches control the Army." I'm only a second lieutenant who has about one year in the Army so discussions on how the Army runs was totally out of my depth. So I said the obvious thing, which was, "Sir, I really don't know how the Army runs." The commander wasn't done and said, "Only stupid people are in the Infantry."

I said to myself, "You have taken a couple of good broadsides and now it's time to make your apology and get out of here," so I responded, "Sir, I never intended to insult you and I apologize. But I joined the Army to be an infantryman. I can't imagine being anything else and I don't apologize for that." At this point, I guess because I didn't breakdown the way my replacement had, he went to the nuclear option and said, "Yes, you're leaving for Germany but let me tell you what is going to happen. I'm your senior rater and when I write your efficiency report you will never be promoted beyond second lieutenant."

"Holy crap!" I thought. "How did this all go so badly? Is there anything I can say to fix this?" Not being quick on my feet, I responded, "That really disappoints me sir but you must do what you think is right." I think he was frustrated that I wouldn't wilt under his attack so he closed the meeting with "You're damn right, I will, now get out."

"Wow, we're done," I thought and responded firmly with "Yes, sir."

I always knew that when you hurt someone's feelings you need to apologize and be sincere in your apology. But it's up to the other person to accept or reject the apology and their decision is out of your control. I would see the mindless animosity between the different branches of the Army many more times during my career.

At this point, I have to explain two things about the Army that lay the foundation for all these stories. Let me do the simple one first. Who are the battalion and depot commanders? Battalion and depot commanders are lieutenant colonels with about twenty years' experience and are selected by a Centralized Competitive Command Selection Board in Washington. Those selected for battalion/depot command are considered to be the top 2–5 percent of the officers eligible.

The second and more complicated subject is the Officer Evaluation System and Promotion System. The shortest way I can say it is that the Army is a very competitive business and it is an "up or out" system. If you are to stay in the Army and retire at

20 years with a pension, you must be promoted on schedule. If you are short of the required 20 years for retirement, too bad for you and for your family. I'm a visual learner so it is easiest to illustrate this as shown below. There are some variables that change year by year but fundamentally this is the program model.

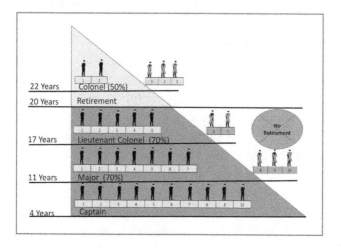

Every illustration falls short so let me try to explain it in words. You can view it like a right triangle. You generally get promoted to captain at four years and then only 60% of captains remaining at the 10 year mark make it to twenty years. The program is designed for 40% of these captains with 10 years invested to be involuntarily released with no pension. A captain with 10 years invested in the service, has to make it through selection to Major at 12 years and then LTC at 17 years to make it to retirement. The Officer Evaluation Report is the primary tool used by promotion boards to decide who stays and who gets released. One bad or poor evaluation report can end your career and put you out before retirement and a pension. It's an old joke but a military career has been described as a "twenty year single elimination basketball tournament".

So I found myself on the bad side of what should be a very qualified depot commander. Sometimes you put your chin out and simply take the punch. (You will also see this again in other stories). In this story, there was no reconciliation with the depot commander and no happy ending. On paper he would appear to be the top 2–5 percent of LTCs but in reality he was a tangled bundle of insecurity, jealousy, and arrogance. You will see in the future stories that my personal experience is that the Army doesn't do very well at selecting senior officers for command.

Was this the worse leader I would fall victim to? I only worked for this man a short time but no, pummeling helpless junior officers only makes him pathetic. The great sin for a commander was still ahead for me.

A few months later the processed Efficiency Report caught up with me in Germany. Happily my rater (a new guy not Joe Omby) had written what he told me he would but the depot commander had also scored me as he had promised. If the selection rate to first lieutenant was 95 percent I was in great jeopardy of missing the cut.

I had no one to help me so I studied the Army regulation governing efficiency reports. This was deep in the last century so there was no internet or phone service back to Korea. I wrote to my old first sergeant who was homesteading in Korea and asked him to send me a copy of the Depot Commander's Assumption of Command Orders. To my relief the orders showed that he had not been in his position the required length of time to qualify as the senior rater on my report (I think it was sixty days). I sent a letter to Officer Records in Washington, DC, with a copy of his orders asking that his evaluation be removed because he didn't meet the time requirement to be a senior rater. Officer records agreed with my argument, they deleted the senior rater portion of the report and doubled the score of the rater portion and happily my career did not end as a second lieutenant. It is probably a little overstatement but basically accurate to say that for my entire career I would go from "hero to zero" with each change of commander.

My next two years in Germany I found myself under a battalion commander who is one of the four finest men I have ever known. How I ended up in his unit was totally out of my control but I suspect that it was God putting me in the exact place I needed to be.

In the commercial world, you also change managers all the time. The ability to change leaders serves as a barometer on the health and resiliency of the organization. The new manager may actually view a situation much differently than his predecessor or sometimes he may only want to discredit him. Suppose you are a "special education teacher" in a public school and your new principle thinks all special education should be done outside of mainstream education. Or suppose you are in sales and handling sensitive negotiations and your new manager thinks the approach pursued by his predecessor was faulty and wants you to do something different. Or suppose you are a department head at a small college competing for the position of dean and when you are not selected, the new dean demotes you back to be a classroom instructor. Sometimes your new manager simply doesn't like you and for any number of reasons wants to torpedo your career. When that happens they normally reorganize and declare you to be excess and you are laid off. It generally doesn't have the finality of being dismissed from the Army because the economy is large and you have options with other companies doing similar work.

To summarize the lessons from my time in Korea: First, now, long out of the Army, it's clear that I benefited most from the instruction provided by Joe Omby. Without his patient instruction I could have easily reached a different and less complete understanding of where minority soldiers are coming from. I think that my time with Joe made me a better company commander, a better manager, a better business owner, a better man and I'm sure that is why God put me under his leadership when he did.

Second, I learned that when speaking in public you have to be sensitive to other people and have some political sense. It can be reckless to be transparent even if you feel you are in a safe place. After this brush with disaster, I committed that any future departing speeches would only contain comments along the lines of how much I appreciated my time in the unit I was leaving.

Third, I learned that you have to tactfully work with senior officers and not expect them to all have the same character or abilities. My experience of having a good commander followed then immediately by a bad commander was a cycle that repeated itself for the next twenty years. I was able to identify the down side of the cycle and with varying success take some defensive measures to survive.

Fourth, I will always remember being in trouble for swapping out the transfer cases on the two wreckers and I think I learned two lessons. One, when I said that "Grace" had been extended to me I mean that senior officers could have simply lowered the boom and destroyed my career, but after looking at all the factors they didn't. Later in my career there were several occasions when I was in the position to extend to junior officers and enlisted soldiers the same grace that I had received. The two that immediately come to mind are the mechanic who rolled my jeep while he was "four wheeling" in the field behind the motor pool and the second lieutenant who rolled the new ammunition forklift. The second lesson was that when you go outside the lines, people come out of the woodwork to criticize you. I was totally befuddled when people not remotely involved in what I was doing rushed to take a moral high ground and condemn me. "You're that lieutenant who doesn't follow regulations," some said to me. "Who are you and what do you know about it?" I would respond. It's funny that a certain type of man will fire shots at you when they think you can't strike back but then they melt instantly when you push back. There was a television commercial in the early 1990s and the punch line was "stay between the lines, the lines are your friend." I find that to be good advice in this instance.

Fifth, you have to bloom where you are planted. Although I wanted to be in the Infantry division it wasn't going to happen and it made no sense to cry about it and sling snot all over everyone. I did the best I could at the jobs I was given.

Sixth, to the extent possible you have to take charge of your career. Because the first depot commander gave me good advice, I asked to go to Germany instead of waiting to see where the Army chose to send me. Deciding on a path and then pursuing it has paid off many times for me.

CHAPTER 3

Professionalism: Money

I arrived in Berlin, Germany, as a second lieutenant. At that time it took two years to be promoted to first lieutenant. After thirteen months in Korea assigned to an Ordnance depot I was delighted to be assigned as an Infantry Rifle platoon leader in a standard Infantry Company. This was critically important because the Infantry platoon leader position is the foundational job to be mastered by an Infantry Officer. The platoon leader has forty soldiers and noncommissioned officers that he is responsible to train, motivate, discipline, and build into a team. This is the closest contact that an officer has with the soldiers and you learn to sense and evaluate their differences in strengths, abilities, desires, aspirations and fears. You learn this through the course of garrison duties including guard details and inspections and then through field training where you conduct weapons qualifications and maneuvers. You learn to read the terrain, anticipate enemy actions, control your unit and coordinate with your supporting fires. The end result is that you are competent in foundational Infantry Weapons and Tactics and can lead your platoon on independent missions as well as part of larger unit maneuvers.

The unit I landed in was totally out of my control and I'm certain that God put me in this unit on purpose. This was an absolutely exceptional unit. My first battalion commander is one of the four finest men I have ever known and I still visit him when I'm in Washington. At his departing dinner, he was asked how he was able to handle the pressures of being a battalion commander on the Russian Front (old cold war slang). His answer went like this, "No matter what pressure I'm feeling, I know that when I look in the mirror I have to answer three questions: Am I a good Christian, am I a good husband and father, and am I a good soldier? If I ensure these priorities guide my decisions, I can face any negative fallout that might come my way." When he said this, it was like a diamond bullet to the brain. It was absolutely clear that this is what we had observed and admired in him for the two years he commanded us. At that time I was not a Christian but I knew that this was how I had to approach my life.

The average officer in this battalion was far above the standard I would observe anywhere at any time the rest of my career. My best friend was a 1LT

Dan Baker and my Company Executive Officer. He was a West Point Graduate and could articulate the "duty-honor-country" value system that I was seeking and wanted to be a part of. "I will not lie, cheat or steal or tolerate anyone who does" was a big part of it. Many of my peers had an IQ 20 points above mine. I remember one first lieutenant who read *Shogun* one night when he had Brigade Guard Detail. At that time, I was reading *The Complete Sherlock Holmes* by Arthur Conan Doyle which 2LT Mike Smith had given me and it took me about six months to finish. So I spent a lot of time watching and seeing what I could learn from these really smart guys. On the down side, although some were brilliant, they also had unbridled ambition. "What's mine is mine and what's yours is mine if I can take it" describes their general outlook. So I took my time finding a comfortable spot in the social fabric of the battalion.

I spent eight months as a Rifle Platoon Leader and then ten months as the Heavy Mortar platoon leader. These were great jobs but the time came for me to rotate into a job as the executive officer for a rifle company. Apart from the tactical and leadership lessons, I became conscious that I lacked some analytical and quantitative skills. I spoke with both my company and battalion commanders about this and they both agreed that I should take some graduate courses at night to improve these skills. I remember the battalion commander saying, "You think just fine, additional schooling will provide the vocabulary to help you express it." In the middle of this I decided that if I could run five miles in a flack jacket with a rifle, that I could run a marathon. I wouldn't run it fast, I would just pace myself. So with two weeks preparation I ran the "Berlin-Spandau Marathon" and fifty kilometers later I felt like every muscle in my body was on fire and I would die. But I was only twenty-three years old and recovered fine with only minor stress fractures in my tibias. My first daughter was also born during this period. Yes, this is Terri my writing coach. Becoming a father changed many aspects of how I viewed the world, but I will discuss those later.

I had been the executive officer for my security company in Korea so the responsibilities in company administration such as supply room, arms room, mail room, nuclear/biological/radiological room were not new to me. Standing in during the company commander's absence was new to me. When the company commander was on leave I was responsible for all the companies activities and would be responsible for administering the Uniform Code of Military Justice (UCMJ) over my soldiers.

I became an executive officer a few weeks before the battalion commander rotated out and we got a new one. This was to play out as a repeat of my experience in Korea and I again went from a great battalion commander to a really poor battalion commander. One of the first things the new commander did was to change the rating schemes for company executive officers. His idea was that the company executive officer would be rated by their company commander but instead of him being the senior rater, we would be rated by the battalion executive officer, a major. The general rule is that rating schemes follow the chain of command so the company executive officer is rated by the company commander and senior rated by the battalion commander. This most excellent idea placed a staff officer who has no control over the company commander at the top of my rating chain. We are all adults and professionals so why is this a bad idea? One example of why this is a bad idea is a situation that arose during one of our training rotations. The battalion was bivouacked in tents in the middle of a German forest for six weeks with each of the five companies assigned their separate area. The battalion executive officer told us company executive officers that he wanted pathways raked between our tents and then lined with stones to make the area look neat. Paint the rocks white if possible. When I laid out my plan to my company commander he said, "No, absolutely not. If we leave today I want the area to be undisturbed—it should look as thou we were never here." So my rater and senior rater were at odds about what they wanted done and I was in the middle. I did what my company commander directed while the battalion executive officer simmered.

At that time the Army had morale and welfare funds named "The Unit Fund." The Unit Fund provided funds for soldier morale activities. These activities were primarily a summer picnic and a Christmas party. These funds were small and accumulated only a couple hundred dollars a year. Traditionally the company executive officer was assigned as the "Unit Funds Officer" and the fund was audited annually for accuracy of accounting and to ensure the funds had been spent on legitimate activities.

I had previously been the Unit Fund Officer for my company in Korea so this was not new to me. One of my first actions was to request an audit of the Unit Fund account. To my surprise I learned that in Germany the Unit Fund Accounts (the accounts of five companies) had recently been merged together at battalion level. Remarkably they hadn't worked out the details of how this consolidation would work. At a high level, each company executive officer was still a Unit Fund Officer for purposes of requesting funds but the funds were now in a pool at battalion level and there was no annual audit. Without an audit this sounded like a big mistake.

I requested to see the general ledger for this new Consolidated Unit Fund. The only expenditure was for $250 and there was no explanation provided for what the funds were spent on. I asked the funds disbursement manager what had been purchased and I was told the battalion executive officer (yes, my senior rater) had withdrawn the funds for a unit party. I had no knowledge of the unit party so I met with battalion executive officer and told him I thought there had been mistake and that we needed to correct it. The major blew me away when he said, "I had to host a reception after the Battalion Commanders Change of Command Ceremony, you were there. I had no source of funds so I took it out of the Unit Fund." I was flabbergasted and responded, "Yes, sir, I was present but only officers attended that reception, the Unit Fund is for the enlisted soldiers." The major was indignant and said, "I wasn't going to pay for it myself. I had no other place to get it." I responded, "But we both know that is a violation of the regulation." The major went on the attack and said, "It's unprofessional for you to question the actions of a superior officer. I'm done discussing it with you, leave now." My well-practiced response was, "Yes, sir."

I went to my company commander and told him about the problem with the funds. He advised me to let it go. So I did nothing.

Some months later, I was moved to the battalion staff as the assistant operations officer and this triggered an efficiency report. To his credit, the battalion executive officer had me into his office and gave me the report in person (there is no requirement for this face to face discussion and most senior raters do not do this). He had scored me down slightly, not enough to hurt me but simply to give me the message that he was in control. He asked if I had any questions about the report so I told him, "Yes, you've marked me down in this section, is there something I should work on?"

He responded, "Yes, you are not flexible, you need to work on this. Primarily you need to understand that sometimes regulations need to be bent and you should never question a senior officer. Frankly I'm not sure you are cut out to be in the Army."

"You rat bastard, I question you about your handling of funds and you declare that I'm unsuited to be an officer" I thought. But instead I said, "Thanks for your candid feedback, do you recommend anything to help me work on this?"

"You should read *Future Shock*, it will make you more flexible," he said. So I read this book. It was a terrific book about technological and social change but had nothing to do with the immediate issues of questionable funds or abuse of position.

The major told me I had no future in the Army solely because he wanted to be mean to me. But in retrospect he was correct in the sense that I would be frustrated throughout my career as I served under bad and corrupt leaders. By good fortune, this major was also rotating out of the unit so although I would be on the staff, he would not be there to rate me again. I was concerned about what he would tell his replacement about me. "Dud, trouble maker, malcontent, poor reader, goes to school at night," all passed through my head. Happily, I got along very well with the new major. My time on the staff was very enjoyable and I grew and developed and found I was more capable then I thought.

So I received another lesson on the perils of antagonizing my senior rater. But that's not what this story is about. The issue is when your superiors do something that is illegal, what do you do? In the commercial world, there are petty cash and impress funds that are vulnerable to this same type of pilferage. What do you do when you discover your boss is dipping into the funds? What do you do when you discover that your boss is taking company materials and equipment home?

Was this the worse leader I would fall victim to? No, playing loose with Army money was not the worse I would see. The great sin for a commander was still ahead for me.

To summarize the lessons from this unit fund adventure: First, I thank God that I don't have a malicious spirit. I am a classic "Type A" personality and I get angry when I feel mistreated or someone hurts my feelings. But understanding that God is ultimately in control of my future helps me keep things in perspective and keeps me from lashing out for the immediate satisfaction it would appear to give. You will see in my future stories that I was provided many opportunities to embrace and refine this prospective.

Second, never, ever as long as you live do anything questionable with money. No amount of money, large or small is worth placing your honesty and honor into question. The questionable handling of such a small amount was simply foolish for this major to do.

Third, sometimes the mere knowledge of the problem requires you to speak out. "I will not lie, cheat, or steal nor tolerate anyone who does." In this case, I didn't think the circumstances were extreme enough for me to go to the mat demanding justice and I believe time has proven this correct. This issue of when to speak out or remain silent will present itself many times in my career.

Fourth, if "Prayer is the last refuge of a scoundrel" then "Professionalism is the last refuge of a senior officer when he is exposed for wrong doing by a junior officer." I don't know who to attribute these sayings to (maybe Lisa Simpson), but I have been given this "professionalism" stiff arm dodge many times even after leaving the Army.

CHAPTER 4

Professionalism Night School

About a year after arriving in Berlin, I realized that I needed to develop better analytical and quantitative skills. There were a couple of American universities with branch campuses such as Boston University that offered graduate programs at night. I discussed the idea of enrolling in a master's degree program with my company commander and later with my battalion commander. They both agreed that if I was willing to sacrifice the time and expense that it would be time well spent. I remember the battalion commander saying, "You think and reason just fine, additional schooling will provide the vocabulary to help you express what you're thinking." So I enrolled in a master's in business administration (MBA) program with Boston University that met two nights a week. Scheduling and attendance were tough but I found that the battalion commander was exactly correct and was surprised that there is an intuitive logic behind subjects like accounting and systems analysis. Our Battalion had about twenty lieutenants and I was the only one doing this.

About the time I had completed three of the eighteen courses, the battalion commander rotated out and our new one rolled in from Washington, DC. So I found myself in a replay of my experience in Korea and I again went from a great battalion commander to a miserably poor battalion commander. This new battalion commander became the source of much personal pain and consequently much material as I write this book. As a poor writer, the challenge is how to break this material into separate stories without boring you with repeating the background information.

Very much to his credit, the new commander had a one-on-one session with each officer in the battalion. In my case, he actually came to my little office and we discussed my experiences in Korea, my experience in this battalion, what my aspirations were. My experience in Korea taught me to be careful about what I said, but I welcomed this opportunity to cultivate an open dialogue with the new commander. The conversation seemed to flow nicely as we discussed that I was going to school at night when my schedule permitted and that I was considering applying for Flight School. There were a number of things happening in the Army that I had to be aware of and navigate through. One of those things was the rumor that the Army was about to extend the promotion point from first lieutenant to captain from four years to four and a half years in service. I told him that this possible change in promotion time to captain was a key point in my deliberations about what I would do next. In brief, if the schedule were left unchanged I would ask to extend in Germany as a new captain and compete for company command. If promotion was moved from four to four and a half years I would ask to leave and go to Flight School while I was still eligible and pursue company command later. He left the meeting telling me that he liked how I had thought things through and that he would support me whichever way circumstances took me. I was extremely happy with how my one-on-one with this new commander had gone. Through no manipulation on my part, he committed that he thought I was a valuable officer, he understood my upcoming career decisions and he committed to support either decision I had outlined. I felt secure that I had a mind meld with the new commander and would not repeat my disastrous departure from Korea.

Now if you are a younger Army person (like under sixty years old), you may be asking, "What is this Flight School discussion all about?" Well that's a story for a later chapter.

The first indication that I totally misread this meeting with the new battalion commander was four months later at a battalion "Officer Professional

Development Class." Actually I hadn't misread the new commander, how can you misread a statement like "I agree with your reasoning and will support your application for Flight School." What I misread was that this commander actual meant what he said and could be relied on to fulfill his commitments. He enjoyed having meetings at the Officers Club which he called "Officer Professional Development Classes." There wasn't much structure to these classes and they were essentially a forum where he would give us his world view on issues and then we would all go to happy hour. During the third of these sessions he was telling us about his previous assignment at the Military Personnel Center (MILPERCEN) and explaining how the selection processes for promotion to LTC and then for battalion command worked. He wanted to be clear that it was harder to be selected for battalion command than it was to simply be promoted to LTC. By now we had observed his self-promotion enough times that we were not surprised that he felt the need to point this out to us.

He was wrapping up his talk when he said almost as an aside, "I don't want you junior officers going to school at night getting master's degrees."

"He didn't really say that?" was my first thought. But he did say it and he blew me away with what he said next: "It is unprofessional for an officer to go to school at night and get a master's degree. I don't have a masters, which proves that you can be a success without one. The Army requires your commitment twenty-four hours a day. If you have free time you should spend it on professional reading."

I was speechless. We had discussed my night classes during my one-on-one and he told me he agreed with me attending night classes. Everyone in the room knew that I was the only lieutenant enrolled in a master's program so we all knew these comments were directed specifically at me. Everyone struggled not to look at me. The awkward silence was broken by one of my friends who asked, "Do you have a list of books that you recommend for us to read?" (Thank you, Sam, Mike, John, whoever asked this question.) The commander answered, "No, but I think I will put a list together." The commander then adjourned the class and we went to happy hour. For the record, he never did provide a professional reading list.

I had learned the lesson in Korea on how different commanders can have vastly different perspectives on the same issue. But this was different because he had personally given me his approval and now he was singling me out in public with the label of "unprofessional." I had paid for the class I was attending so I wasn't going to drop it but I was in a quandary as to whether to drop out of the program at the end of this class. Shortly after this embarrassing public statement of admonishment, I was moved to the battalion staff as assistant operations officer. For the remainder of my time in Germany, I spent so much time away from garrison that it was impractical to attend classes so going to night school was no longer an issue.

Was this the worse leader I would fall victim to? No, calling out junior officer for a public admonishment was not the worse I would see. The great sin for a commander was still ahead for me and this commander will simply provide more material for this book.

In the commercial world bad managers are also happy to expound on what they think their subordinates should or should not do after work. What do you do if your manager tells you that working in the church food pantry is foolishness because people should be able to take care of themselves? Does your continued work at the food pantry impact your promotion potential? Do you continue or do you put it on hold and see what happens?

To summarize the lessons from this "Professionalism-Night School" adventure first, you have to be prepared that leaders will change their minds or not follow through on their agreements. Despite a very clear agreement on my attending night school, this commander reversed himself and left me hanging.

Second, you have to take responsibility for your career and do the things you see as necessary. You have to be prepared that your managers might disagree with your choices.

Third, You also have to have some political sense. Sometimes you have to look at the longer game and silently acquiesce to the peculiarities of your leaders. When they put you on notice with a clear statement of their expectations, you have to weigh the risk vs. reward of not complying.

Fourth, applying this lesson later to managing the contracts for my company I have coined the phrase "the government contracting officer is always right—even when they are wrong, try to make them right." For example, sometimes they ask for pricing data they are not entitled to but if it facilitates them awarding a contract to me, I bite my tongue and say "of course I will give it to you. I can work on it tonight. Is it okay if it's in your inbox when you arrive in the morning?" On another occasion, I was told, "I don't like the format of your invoices, it looks like you bought some cheap invoicing software, I want it changed." I pushed back and said, "Yes, I bought an affordable software program that meets the requirements of the Defense Finance and Accounting Agency and I will continue to use it."

CHAPTER 5

Pilots Get Paid More Than I Do

Deep into my assignment in Berlin, I was a first lieutenant and the assistant battalion operations officer for an Infantry battalion. I had enjoyed two years under a battalion commander who was simply one of the four finest men I have ever known. He was replaced by a man with not only less intellectual and leadership ability but quickly proved to also possess less moral fiber and character.

In my previous story "Professionalism and Night School," I told about my initial one-on-one meeting with the new commander and receiving his blessing and endorsement of my career plans which might or might not involve Flight School. For continuity in the story let me briefly say that when he first took command he meet with me one-on-one asked me what my near term aspirations were. I told him that the pending change in promotion time to captain was a key consideration. My plan was that if the schedule were left unchanged I would ask to remain in Germany as a captain and compete for company command. If it were extended from four to four and a half years I would ask to go to Flight School while I was still eligible and pursue company command later. He responded that he thought this was a good plan and would support it.

In that story I promised that later in this book I would explain the details of how the Army managed Flight School back in the last century. That explanation follows now. If you are a younger Army person (like under sixty years old), you may be asking "what is this Flight School discussion all about?" The Aviation Branch was not created until 1982. Prior to that, all Officers belonged to another branch and Aviation was simply a secondary specialty. The primary branches with Aviation requirements were Infantry, Armor, Field Artillery, Transportation, Military Intelligence, Signal and Medical. Many second lieutenants went to Flight School right after their basic officer course and did a flight assignment before being assigned to their owning branch. But for most, they had an initial assignment in their branch and then went to Flight School as a first lieutenant or junior captain. For officers in this second group, you had to start Flight School before the end of your first five years (sixty months) of service.

I hoped that as an Infantry Aviator, that I would spend my career in Infantry Divisions by alternating assignments between Infantry and Aviation Units. I would be a full time field officer and not spend time in Recruiting Command, Reserve Components and Reserve Officer Training Corps (ROTC) or Washington, DC. Although not an enticement to me, Aviators also receive flight pay. Flight pay is a specialty pay of a couple of hundred dollars per month as an incentive to keep aviators from leaving the service. I believe there are a number of similar incentives in place today, maybe for cyber security.

Shortly after I was moved to the battalion staff, the Army changed the time in service for promotion to captain from four to four and a half years. Having planned for this possibility, I immediately applied for Flight School. When you apply for a major program like Flight School, Graduate School, or Language School, the application process requires that your battalion commander endorse it with approval or disapproval before it goes to MILPERCEN. Whether I would be accepted for Flight School was unknown but since I had already discussed this with the commander and had his agreement, I didn't expect any problems at our end. My application for Flight School went into the battalion commander's office and entered a black hole. I heard nothing for several weeks and the adjutant, who controlled the flow of these actions, would only tell me that the application was on the battalion commander's desk.

After several weeks, I asked for a meeting with the battalion commander to request that he move my request forward and the dialogue went like this: Commander: "Lieutenant you are a good Infantry officer and you will be wasted in Aviation."

I responded, "Thank you, sir, I appreciate that evaluation but I'm confused. We have discussed this before. We discussed that if the promotion zone for captain was moved to four and a half years, that I would apply for Flight School and you said you would endorse it." The commander wasn't willing to acknowledge our previous discussions and said, "We need junior officers like you here."

"Son of a bitch," I thought, "he's not going to endorse this. My only chance is to stay on point that he has agreed to this," so I said, "Sir, you agreed that you would support my request, I don't see that anything has changed."

The commander still didn't want to go that route and he tried to change the subject by saying, "If you look at the brigade's rotation roster you will see that we are going to be short captains, which means that senior lieutenants like yourself will be given company commands for the first time."

This was true, but only partly true. Yes, it appeared that there may opportunities for a first lieutenant to slip into a company command but there was no reason to believe that I would be that lucky first lieutenant. We had several first lieutenants in the brigade who had either a father, or a father-in-law who was still on active duty as a general officer and I'm not naive enough to believe that this battalion commander would pass up the chance to endear himself to a general by sponsoring his son to a company command. Heck he regularly played golf with two generals sons. But if he wants to entice me with visions of being the only first lieutenant to command in the brigade I should at least enter into the discuss so I asked the best question I could think of, "Sir, are you offering me a company command?" The commander responded with open aggravation, "No, I'm just saying that you should extend here and maybe you will score a company command." Okay, I thought, he's simply trying to distract me with a promise that isn't really a promise so now I have to get back on message, "Sir, I appreciate that possibility but I think the best thing to do is to go to Flight School while I can. I would like you to fulfill your commitment to me and endorse my application." Now he gave me his meanest, darkest scowl, and said, "Okay, look, I don't want you to go be an aviator because they get flight pay and I don't."

"Unbelievable," I thought. Until now I had thought he was just a jerk who wanted to keep me in his unit and milk my abilities as long as he could but now I see the same twisted insecurity and jealousy that I had seen in the Ordnance commander I reported in my "I'm Too Smart to Be an Infantryman" story.

I must stop now and say, on behalf of every competent and psychologically balanced Infantry officer in the Army, there is no sweeter sound short of heaven, then the sound of US Army helicopters coming over the ridge to support you. If you have never read Hal Moore's book *We were Soldiers Once and Young*, the movie doesn't count—you have to read that book. Put my story aside and read that book first. The first time I read it I was an Aviation LTC and I cried and my wife asked, "What on earth are you crying about?" For the purpose of my story, although LTC Moore was the quarterback of that classic Infantry/Aviation/Artillery victory, Major Bruce Crandall the Aviation Company Commander was also a hero. Major Crandall was a hero not just for his aviation skills but because of his ability to think ahead of the battle, getting ahead of the decision cycle, anticipating what Moore would need and pushing water, ammunition, Medivac forward on his own initiative. So for an Infantry battalion commander to resent Army Aviators because of flight pay is simply asinine.

How did he ever get selected to battalion command? But I was a lieutenant who was now in a fight with my battalion commander over my desire to be an Infantry Aviator so I responded the best I could, "Sir, flight pay is not my motivation. I want to command both Infantry and Aviation units. Again, we have discussed this before and you told me you would support this before the window closes and I'm no longer eligible. I'm asking you to please, honor your promise to endorse my application" The commander was furious but said, "Okay, I will endorse it. Now get out!" My response was, "Thank you, sir," and I left not knowing if he would actually do it or if I would have to request a second meeting.

My application sat on the commander's desk for two more weeks and the adjutant, who was on the Commander's Golf Team, told me to quit asking about it. We were told he was going on a two-week vacation so I took a risk and told the battalion executive officer (my senior rater) about my problem. He spoke with the commander and urged him that if he had made a commitment to me, that he probably needed to honor it. The commander went on leave without signing it.

With the commander on leave the executive officer was legally the "acting commander" and had authority to sign my application. He wrote a strong endorsement and told me two things—first, "if I need helicopter support, you are exactly the person I want to support me." And second, "When you are a commander, don't ever fail to fulfill the commitments you make to your men." I was then fortunate and I received orders for Flight School. I was also fortunate that the battalion commander was not my senior rater and I did not take a hit on my efficiency report. The executive officer was very much a Hal Moore type and very much wanted tactically competent Aviation commanders.

This battalion had regular parties where the officers and wives met to welcome the new people and acknowledge the people departing. I learned from the mistake I made when I left Korea so when I was asked to share some departing remarks, I was gracious and told everyone how much I appreciated what I had learned from each of them.

Shortly after I left for Flight School, this battalion commander did give a company command to a first lieutenant. This lucky first lieutenant played on the commander's golf team and was also the son of an active duty brigadier general. In full disclosure, I do not present that I was better qualified to be a company commander then he was. First of all I'm sure that he was a better reader and writer then I was. The point I'm trying to make is that the commander attempted to entice me with a company command he had no intention of giving me and luckily I did not take the bait.

Was this the worse leader I would fall victim to? No, refusing to honor a commitment and jerking around a junior officer was not the worse I would see. The great sin for a commander was still ahead for me and this commander simply provides more material for this book.

To summarize the lessons from this "Pilots Get Paid More Than I Do" adventure, first, this animosity toward officers in other career fields was not new to me and I could look forward to seeing it many more times. I have a brother who was an Army Finance Corp officer. He thought the combat arms officers were absolutely foolish for taking the risks and hardships inherent with the combat arms. I frankly appreciated that Finance Branch paid me correctly and I never resented them for not facing the discomforts and separations of field duty. But in this case, I was amazed and I suppose glad that the commander would be transparent and actually tell me what his problem was.

Second, when you make a commitment to a subordinate you are obligated to do your best to fulfill that commitment. In my case I'm sure that the commander had no intention of endorsing my application and if he had not gone on leave, I would have not gone to Flight School. I don't think I would have handled that very well.

Third, all people join an organization (Army or company) looking for opportunity. To deny your subordinates opportunities they are qualified to pursue because of your own petty prejudices is both unprofessional and in this case unbecoming of a commanding officer.

CHAPTER 6

Canadians Don't Speak French

I grew up on the Canadian Border. Sault Ontario was a three-mile drive across the International Bridge. This is a two-lane bridge, which is the only crossing for 250 miles in either direction so it is frequently congested with a thirty-minute wait to get through US Customs. Canadian customs never seem to take very long, unless they think you've been drinking. We have a "Bridge Walk" every July to celebrate the close relationship between our two communities. I think it is really to celebrate the fact that we have the bridge and for those who can remember, it is one thousand, no one million percent better than the old automobile ferry system. Anyway the walk starts on the American side at the Lake Superior State College

Hockey Rink and on the Canadian side you gather at the Casino and ride a school bus back. When I was young I would jog across and later I would walk with my family and sometimes push a baby in a stroller. Now that I'm old I get frustrated waiting for the bus back which usually takes longer than the three-mile walk so I don't do it anymore. Maybe this is symptom of "cranky old man's syndrome."

Before cable TV came to our area in the late 1960s, Channel 2 from Sault Ontario was our only source of television. Channel 2 was a Canadian Broadcasting Corporation (CBC) station, which had some affiliation with the American operated Columbia Broadcasting System (CBS) so although most programing was Canadian, we did see Bonanza and the Ed Sullivan Show on Sunday nights. Without Ed Sullivan we would have totally missed out on "Beatle Mania." "Hockey Night in Canada" and "Floyd Robertson with the National News" were the two most important Canadian programs. Consequently I was better versed on what was happening with Rene Levesque and the Quebec Sovereignty Movement then I was with Eldridge Cleaver and the Black Panther Party. Even now I suspect that anyone back home reading this will ask, "Who was Eldridge Cleaver?" So the point is that I grew up familiar with Canada.

During my time in the Army, this Canadian connection was quint, but not important. Actually some people thought my lack of US television knowledge made me a little "culturally stinted."

"How can you not know what Soul Train is, did you grow up on Mars?" some would ask. Sometime I would be at a party and someone would ask, "Hay, are you the Canadian guy?"

"No," I would answer. "Oh darn, I've never met a Canadian so I was hoping that you were one." For myself, I always wanted to meet someone from Maine and after ten years in the Army, I finally met one. "What did your father do for work, I mean how did he earn a living?" I asked. "He did a little bit of everything—painted houses, worked some farming, worked the fishing boats, mostly tried to keep us in winter cloths waiting for summer to come," he told me. So I understood that this family struggled to stave off poverty just like mine in Michigan. Another common question people asked me was "You're a hockey player, right? Good, so what exactly is icing the puck anyway?"

"No one really knows but we know it when we see it" was my usual response.

My Canadian connection caused me some surprising pain one time when I was a lieutenant in Germany. I was the assistant operations officer in an Infantry battalion and enjoying the job immensely. I liked the pace. I liked the analysis and the planning processes. I liked running the operations center during maneuvers. The pace was fast and I operated four radios and two were encrypted secure. I liked writing the operations orders, you know "Second Battalion attacks Hill223 at 0700, Company A on the left and Company B on the Right, Company C in reserve, Mortars in General Support, etc.," really good Army stuff. "Who feeds the Recon Platoon?" Company B, it's in paragraph 4 of the Ops Order I would respond.

My problem occurred while we were on a six week rotation at a major training area on the East German Border and were sharing the facilities with a Canadian Unit, the Royal Twenty-Second Regiment. They are from Quebec and their nickname is the "Van Doos" which is the English pronunciation of the French word for 22. Their Cap Badge includes a Beaver and their motto "Je me souviens" which is the official motto of Quebec. As the Assistant Operations Officer I attended daily meetings with the "Van Doos" when we coordinated range scheduling. I was a uniquely good fit for this because I knew all about the Stanley Cup, the Memorial Cup, the Gray Cup and I was conversant in all of the teams in both the Ontario and Quebec Junior Hockey Leagues. Just as importantly I also knew to avoid any conversation about the renegade Rene Levesque because he might be related to some of these guys.

One morning in the third week, I entered the operations center and a sergeant called out from across the room, "Maj de Gaulle from the Van Doos wants you to call him." I carelessly responded "I hope he speaks English." This was really silly because they were all bilingual in French and English, but we joked about what we might have to do if we ran across someone who only spoke French so this comment did make some sense.

At this point, the battalion commander announced his presence. He had been sitting in the corner watching things and I hadn't noticed him. The commander barked, "Lieutenant, stand at attention, I want to talk to you." I was thinking, what the hell is this about but I came to attention and said, "Yes, sir."

"What did you say, Lieutenant?" he asked.

"I hope he speaks English, sir," I responded. "Of course he speaks English, what else would he speak?" he fired back.

"French, sir," I responded with my best authoritative voice. Heck, I knew exactly what I was talking about so he must be testing me to see how I work under pressure and I think this authoritative tone will be good. "Canadians don't speak French you idiot," he lashed out. There was a dreadful, no a painful silence. "The commander has been drinking early today," was my next thought. Everyone wanted to leave the building but no one wanted to be the first to move. Then the operations officer, my boss and a major came to my defense and said, "Sir, the lieutenant is from up there and he knows about Canada."

"So you're from up there?" the commander said faking curiosity but we all knew it was sarcasm. I thought that if I gave a complete answer that I could defuse the situation and responded, "Yes, sir, I grew up on the border and in fact my grandmother was French Canadian from Three Rivers Quebec." I'm not quick on my feet and I was really proud of that answer and thought I had ended the discussion.

But I was wrong because the commander said, "So your grandmother was French Canadian, so do you speak French?"

"No, sir," I responded.

"Well, that proves it," the commander said.

"That proves what, sir?" I asked now in total confusion. "That Canadians don't speak French, you idiot!" he said, now showing that he visibly aggravated with me. I could see that I had to get out of this discussion so I said, "Yes, sir, I see you are right, that does prove it."

With his well-earned and now very public victory in hand the commander applied the coup de grace or head shot but saying, "Don't be saying ignorant foolish things any more, Lieutenant," I responded sheepishly, "Yes, sir." My sheepishness was a really good tactic as it cemented for him this total victory, kind of like his own VE Day. Sometimes you have to step back and accept that there is no point in continuing the discussion and this was one of those times. Yes it was humiliating, I suppose like a child getting a bare bottom spanking in public. Ouch!

The next week, the commander crashed a party at the Canadian NCO Mess and entertained them by drinking beer out of his boot. I guess that was his best attempt at pursuing international and cross cultural understanding. I never asked him what language they were speaking.

So how does a man rise to this level of leadership and have such a total lack of understanding about Canada? But for the point of this book, how does he rise to this level of command and humiliate junior officers this way? Actually I was lucky because he didn't "fine" me. During our next training rotation, he got mad at another lieutenant and told him he was "fining him $200." He directed the lieutenant to send $200 to his alma mater and bring him the receipt or he would face trouble. Of course this extortion was totally illegal. Our take-home pay was about $400 a month so $200 was a lot of money but it was a small amount to pay to avoid having your career ended by a Battalion Commander playing a power game. My friend did as he was told and the Virginia Military Institute received his $200 donation to the general scholarship fund.

I thank God that this was not my first battalion commander. Half the new officers leave the Army after their initial obligation is up at three to five years. Many simply have no interest in a career and leave feeling they had positive experiences. But many fall into a bad unit and think this is what the whole Army is like so they quit. As one departing lieutenant told me, "I've seen the monkey show and I want nothing to do with it."

But there are some downstream consequences for an event like this. One bad consequence is that when subordinates see their leaders treated with contempt by the senior commanders, it creates an air of disdain and makes it difficult to lead some of them. One happy consequence of this bare bottom spanking was the outrage expressed by some of my friends and the fact that it still lives on for them. There was joking that we should change our battalion motto from "Unity is Strength" to "Canadians don't speak French" or maybe "You're an idiot" or more generically "Someone's an idiot." I still communicate with friends from that unit and about once a year I will get a phone call from one of them. Usually it's in November and they just heard "The Wreck of the Edmond Fitzgerald" on the radio and they start the conversation with the question "Do Canadians still speak French?" Some have proposed that I put "Canadian's Don't Speak French" on my tombstone and if this book gets published I expect to see this question on Facebook.

Not related to my problem but funny enough to mention is that during this period the commander introduced the concept of "The Round Table." He had a couple of folding tables cut to fit into a round GP Small Tent. He could fit eight people around the table and have one of the cooks serve the food. While this was being played out the other officers and men would be eating their dinner huddled from the rain under a poncho. Navy guys will simply not understand why this is strange but for the Army it was remarkably poor leadership. It is so bad that it was made part of the leadership curriculum at the Infantry Officer Advance Course at Ft. Benning. When I attended, one of the classes in the leadership block provided examples of really stupid bad leadership and "The Round Table" had made its way into this list of dubious leadership mistakes. Sometime I can look at my mistakes and take solace that "at least I'm not part of the curriculum at Ft. Benning"

A few years later, I was in a Company Commander's Pre-command course at the Ninth Infantry Division at Ft. Lewis Washington. One of the instructors approached me and said, "I know you from Germany, you're the Canadian hockey player."

"Well, no, I'm not Canadian but forgive me because I don't remember you sir," I answered. "I don't think we ever met but I knew who you were. I was as a major at brigade headquarters and you were a lieutenant working for Colonel Charming down in the Second Battalion," he said.

"Yes, sir, that all tracks but in full disclosure I have to tell you that although I worked for him, I'm not a fan of the colonel," I replied. His face suddenly grew stern and he asked, "You didn't like the colonel?"

"Let's just say that our leadership approaches are very different and I simply had trouble working for him," I said. Then his face relaxed into a smile and he said, "I'm glad to hear this. At brigade we all saw him as a drunken buffoon and wondered what it was like serving under him and how many junior officers he was ruining. It is clear that you fought through it," he said.

"Oh, I don't know if you are aware but Colonel Charming is no longer in the Army." He added, "No I had no idea. After leaving that unit I never kept track of him," I replied. This was not completely true because although I never inquired about him as you see I still chaff over the Canadians don't speak French and other misdeeds I lay at his feet. "Well," the major then explained "after commanding your battalion he came to work at headquarters and there were problems with driving under the influence and the general told him to retire or face court-martial." I flashed back to seeing him fall out of his jeep drunk during a training exercise and my driver whispering to me "that's why officers have drivers."

I responded to the major with, "I guess that was bound to happen." We agreed to get together and discuss some unspecified things about Germany but we never ran into each other again. I never did anything to followup on the accuracy of the major's report.

Was this the worse leader I would fall victim to? No, calling out junior officer for public humiliation was not the worse I would experience. This commander provided much material for this book but the great sin for a commander was still ahead for me.

To summarize the lessons from this "Canadians Don't Speak French" adventure. Yes, I still carry the scar tissue from that bare bottom spanking and I guess it's reasonable. It's amazing how hurts and injuries never really leave me alone. I know that I'm not alone and everyone has this problem. These memories come out of nowhere like when I simply hear a song on the radio that triggers a bad memory. At its most ludicrous extreme, I can be praying and something from the past will come out of nowhere to distract me and I have to ask myself, "Where did that even come from?" How stupid and what a waste of emotional energy to let these thoughts occupy my mind for one instance. When this happens I ask God to forgive my immaturity and simply flush these thoughts out of my head. In the case of "Canadian's don't speak French," I do get a lot of comic relief out of sharing the story. Heck, I'm laughing as I write this.

CHAPTER 7

Cry Baby

This is one of the chapters I didn't want to write. If you're not interested in what causes me pain, skip this chapter.

The stewardess came through the cabin of the airplane asking everyone to close their window shades so they could show a movie. It was a Military Airlift Command charter bringing us back from a deployment to Saudi Arabia in 1994. I went over on a thirty-six-hour flight in the back of an Air National Guard C-141 cargo plane with the spare parts so this commercial Boeing 747 was an absolute luxury. Gulf War One was two years in the past and Sadum Hussan was acting up so we deployed with an Infantry Division in October. It was a foolish deployment because we all knew that after the beatdown he received in February 1991 that he was not a real threat to attack again. We also knew that he was simply rattling our cage and having us spend hundreds of millions of dollars deploying twenty thousand soldiers and shipping thousands of tanks, artillery and helicopters to defend against an attack he was never going to launch. I was a LTC so although I knew this, I could never say it out loud. Although I saw no possibility that we would be in combat, I had my game face on and made sure that I was 100 percent prepared for any action that might occur and said nothing that might undermine the readiness or morale of our unit.

When I arrived I met a friend named LTC Mike Buckley. We first met when we were captains at the Infantry Advance Course at Ft. Benning Georgia. After Gulf War I, when he commanded a tank unit in the First Infantry Division, Mike found himself in what to me was a very exciting job. He was the point man for Army deployments to Africa and the Middle East. In this job he was the first man into country when the Army deployed. For example he was the first man into Somalia and now he was the first man back into Saudi Arabia. Mike normally reported to the US Embassy and then coordinated the arrival of our troops and equipment. He never said this but I think this particular deployment was a nightmare for him.

This deployment involved sending an Infantry Division, which would then fall in on equipment, which we had prepositioned on a small fleet of "roll-on, roll-off" ships that were maintained in the

Indian Ocean at Diego Garcia. The equipment had been placed on the ships a year earlier from a Division being withdrawn from Europe. That withdrawal was celebrated by bands playing as the ships sailed away and awards for all the senior officers.

Mike's problems started the moment the first ship arrived. The last tank to be loaded and now the first to be off loaded had no engine. Yes, the rat bastards that loaded it winched it onboard to meet the celebration schedule and now it was a sixty-ton plug blocking anything coming off the ship. Mike reported the problem back to Washington. You can imagine the consternation as a number of officers who were still polishing the awards they received for loading the equipment in Germany declared that he was lying. Today we could simply take a cell phone photo and text it but back then we had no internet so he was stuck trying to get his message out by telephone and fax machine. Because we were young and willing to take risks and because we wanted to get the operation moving, we agreed to let a soldier "free wheel' it with no power off the ship. All went well and we began the offloading.

Then Headquarters sent three senior officers who outranked Mike to take charge and get things moving. What a travesty. They were all smart guys but had no idea on how to get things moving and worse yet were each undercutting each other in their reports back home. You know the language "I'm the only one here making things happen, I should have been sent sooner, yes it will be difficult but I can turn this mess around."

Like myself, Mike was twenty minutes short of retirement and was looking for a job outside the Army. So he was able to let this nonsense roll off his back and quietly gave directions so the offloading could proceed. He also had a brief exchange with the Deploying Division staff when they complained that "there are no radio's in these tanks."

"Well no, sir," Mike told them, "page 113 of the deployment plan requires that you bring your radios with you." So we had to get everyone to read the plan. Then we found countless errors with the inventory of the supply containers. For example Container 12345 was listed as mortar ammunition but when we opened it we found camouflage nets. It became obvious that our deployment may serve to provide entertainment for the Iraq's but would allow us to shake out our problems and get everything repaired, repackaged and loaded correctly.

I thought I would be the last man from my unit out of the country. I proposed this in our morning staff meeting and the colonel who was now running things (he called himself the chief of staff) said, "You're damn right you are."

"Nice that he agrees with you but his enthusiasm is a little over the top," Mike whispered to me.

As we approached the end of the mission the chief of staff correctly turned his focus on planning for our unit to return to the US. Remarkably, the central and most critical part of his planning was a commitment he had made to our general back in the US that he would have a certain number of people on the first flight home so the general could meet them and host a reception at the airfield. This reception included an Army Band, flags waving and speeches and the most important photo op such as "General welcomes heroes home." Since I would go home the way I arrived, this planning didn't interest me.

Unfortunately for our chief of staff, but fortunate for me, our organization included a large number of contractors whom the colonel had no real control over. They were not under the Code of Military Justice and had the latitude to catch a commercial flight home and every morning we found that more had disappeared. Kind of like Bedouins slipping away in the night, they would secretly make a plane reservation and hit the road. The colonel demanded that those remaining surrender their passports to him but this was an empty demand and they simply laughed at him.

So the day the first airplanes arrived, the colonel was scrambling to find enough people to fill the plane and provide the general with the photo opportunity that he had promised. So that is how/why I, designated as the last man out of country, became one of the first men out of the country. Yes, in our morning staff meeting the chief of staff ran the numbers and told me to get on the plane that night. "Okay, if that's what you want," I told him. What I was really thinking was "Yuck, I'm going to be a prop for a miserable photo op but at least I'm getting away from this idiot."

The movie they showed on the plane was *Forest Gump*. I had heard of this movie but not seen it. The movie is based on a high-performing autistic fictional character who through a series of bizarre circumstances finds himself in the middle of key events and interacting with key people of the 1960s–1970s. Presidents Kennedy, Johnson, Nixon and Alabama Football Coach Bear Bryant to name a few. It was entertaining and light hearted until the point when Gump goes to Vietnam. At this point I suddenly felt emotional. I cleared my throat to suppress any clue that I was having an emotional response to the movie. There were similar sounds from the dark around me. We were all glad that it was dark so we could wipe our eyes while pretending we were blowing our noses or cleaning our glasses.

When the movie ended everyone lined up at the bathrooms. It's an old cliché but if Army guys do anything well it is standing in line. Everyone was looking at their feet because they didn't want anyone to see their puff eyes. How ashamed everyone felt. When these men left their families and deployed, it included the possibility that they could not return until they had fought a land campaign. Happily that had not happened. So now these men felt unworthy and ashamed. They felt ashamed that having not engaged in combat, that they could be moved to tears by a stupid movie that wasn't even true. We all felt the shame and everyone knew not to discuss it.

It is a code in the Army that officers always eat last and that is a good code. Unfortunately, it also means that sometimes officers go to the bathroom last. Oh my goodness, standing in line, clinching my thigh muscles and pretending I wasn't on the verge of wetting my pants. "Oh no, Private, you go next, I can wait."

"God, please help me to hold this." It seemed like I waited forever and my teeth hurt from grinding them together. During that wait my friend Mike and I found ourselves together in line. I thought it was safe talking with him about the movie so I said, "What did you think of the movie?"

"Oh, I slept and didn't watch it," he replied.

"It was a good movie," I told him.

"What a liar," I thought.

"It's a sixteen-hour flight and this is the only entertainment, of course you watched it." But I knew that after all he saw in Gulf War I and Somalia that he was still ashamed of getting emotional over a movie and simply didn't want to discuss it.

I was always an emotional child. I was cursed with the worse combination of being hopelessly sentimental and perhaps emotionally fragile. These emotions meant that I was frequently called a cry baby. Usually I was called this by my sisters because they knew my parents would slap me silly if I hit them. This sentimentality played itself out in many ways. I would cry when a movie would make me feel the sad emotions of one of the characters. A movie could make me cry when a character lost a loved one like his mother. I would slip into thinking how I would feel if I lost my mother. Pets were never a big deal to me but I cried when "Old Yeller" died because it broke "Travis's" (the boy star) heart. So maybe you don't know who Old Yeller is but maybe you remember a 1970s TV movie *Brian's Song* about the friendship between Chicago Bears football players when one died of cancer. If you don't know what I'm talking about you can Google them or just forget it.

I think being emotional maybe a psychological thing while fighting maybe more of an intellectual thing. So I can separate them this way. When I was a sixteen-year-old hockey player I would fight at the drop of a hat because that was part of the game. I never took it personally or felt bad about it. In tenth grade I got ejected from a high school football game for starting a fight. I did it because I thought it would give my team an emotional lift. When the coach talked to me after the game he explained that he understood that fighting was allowed in hockey and why I might do it but he was coaching football and I was not to do that again. Okay for me, just a different game with different rules. But being able to take a punch was different than being disarmed by feeling emotional pain. I could easily tell someone "You broke my nose" but I could never tell someone "you broke my heart." No, emotions are the hardest things to defend against.

If you are leading Infantry soldiers and they sense that you are emotional or sentimental they will eat you alive. So when I became an Infantry lieutenant, I had to bury this sentimentality. I had to bury it deep. I established a persona as stern, self-controlled, fact driven and ultimately the meanest man on the battle field. I was a no nonsense commander and I never raised my voice or showed emotion but when required I could stare down the toughest non-commissioned officers. It was a facade but it allowed me to shield my emotions both from my soldiers and also from my senior leaders.

When I was a captain, I commanded along with a major who I subsequently worked for and I love to this day. When I worked for him, he related an event from the previous week where someone had attacked him in a meeting and hurt his feelings. I was amazed. I had never heard an officer volunteer that his feelings had been hurt. It seemed somehow freeing that you could acknowledge that your feelings were hurt and to then move on. I embraced this idea and over the years have found there were situations where I could defuse a volatile conversation simply by saying, "You did this to hurt me and it hurt my feelings. Now I've told you and gotten it off my chest and we can move on with what has to be done."

Now I'm an old man and I cry like an old woman. This is terribly embarrassing. I'm asked to speak at funerals and I have to say no because it is uncomfortable both for me but also for the people who will be held prisoner in their seats. I have asked God to help me with this. "Lord," I have asked, "please bring back Captain Rick the Company Commander and get rid of this whimpering old woman." So far this is an unanswered prayer.

I have two granddaughters who are five and six years old, one in Minnesota and one in Vermont. They both worship me and when they visit we frequently listen to music together. Last Christmas we were listening to the "Shrek" version of Leonard Cohen's song "Hallelujah." You know the song "I heard there was a secret chord, that David played that pleased the Lord..." I teared up and they asked, "Why does this song make you cry?"

"Because it makes me happy, it makes me feel like I'm close to God" I told them. My daughters have separately reported that when they hear this song somewhere the granddaughters will say, "This is the song that makes grandpa cry because it makes him feel happy and close to God."

I think that maybe Forest Gump in his transparency also communicates a closeness with God.

To summarize this admission on being a cry baby, what is it about crying that makes me so conflicted? Somehow we can empathize when players and coaches cry in both winning and losing championships and say, "Go ahead and cry, it's part of the experience." But then we don't accept someone crying at a movie or even a funeral. When I was a commander and had soldiers and friends die, I didn't cry in public because I was the leader. I waited and cried in private with my wife. As much as I hate that I cry, I think it must be important and I hope everyone has something that can make them cry and hopefully feel closer to God.

CHAPTER 8

If They Can't Fly I Want Their Wings

I was out of Flight School ten months when I was given command of the headquarters company in the division aviation battalion. The commanders of the other four companies were majors.

Eight months later, I gave up the headquarters company and replaced one of the majors and was now a captain commanding a 22-ship, 150-man Aviation Company in an Infantry Division. I could not believe my good luck. I had six each of the UH-1 Iroquois (Huey) and sixteen each of the OH-58A Kiowa.

The UH-1 was the Army's utility work horse from 1960 to 1990. It had a pilot and co-pilot and had sufficient instrumentation to allow it to conduct instrument flight under Instrument Flight Rules (IFR). Instrument Flight means flying with no outside visual references and relying totally on the instruments in the cockpit. Instrument flight in a these old helicopters had a tremendous workload and required two pilots. The Army requires two pilots for IFR flights even in todays modern helicopters.

The OH-58A was the primary light utility helicopter from 1969 until it was upgraded to OH-58C in the mid-1980s. It was the unfortunate result of the "lowest price source selection process." It was a single pilot helicopter and was not instrumented for IFR operations. It was grossly under powered and although it had seats for the pilot plus three passengers, it was routinely limited to the pilot plus only one passenger. It also had an underperforming tail rotor which caused a problem known as "loss of tail rotor effectiveness." This meant that at low speeds such as takeoff, landing, or essentially anytime you were close to the ground, the tail rotor might not produce sufficient thrust to maintain controlled flight and the aircraft would spin out of control and crash. By 1980 the Army was reporting that 40 percent of all OH-58 crashes were the result of this problem. To avoid the "loss of tail rotor effectiveness," we trained our pilots to perform their takeoffs and landings faster than the published flight standards.

The battalion commander was one of the four finest men I've ever known. Under his leadership our battalion fielded a company of new AH-1 Fully Modernized Cobras and after training they were spun off to form a new attack helicopter battalion. This was followed immediately by fielding the divisions first UH-60 Blackhawk company. Then we reorganized under a new Aviation Brigade Structure with six battalions for a Department of the Army Directed Force Modernization Test Bed. Fielding these new units and immediately reorganizing was a tremendously complex task. I never met another officer with the leadership, technical and management skills and the temperament needed to accomplish it. His selfless character was second to none and it was evidenced in the many gut wrenching decisions I saw him make.

This new Aviation Brigade was commanded by a full colonel. About six months under this new organizational structure, the word circulated that the brigade commander had not been selected for promotion to brigadier general. Whether the colonel got promoted to general had nothing to do with my little world as a captain company commander. At least that's what I thought. But I was wrong. Almost immediately he began firing his battalion commanders. You may remember from my earlier explanation that battalion commanders were essentially the top 2–5 percent of all lieutenant colonels. The first victim was my battalion commander and within six months he had fired two more. I never understood why no one higher in the chain of command ever questioned how so many battalion commanders (50 percent) could be such poor performers that they should be fired. The command atmosphere became toxic and a pattern immediately emerged. When one battalion commander got fired, a surviving battalion commander of another unit would fire one of his company commanders in an effort to take pressure off himself. Predictably, each new battalion commander was determined not to suffer the same fate as his predecessor and they began by showing everyone that they could produce results and correct bad performance.

So we got our new battalion commander and once again I was repeating the cycle of a good commander being replaced by a poor commander. I was now three for three. Since he was replacing a commander who had been sacked and run out of town in disgrace, he had no hesitation in openly ridiculing his predecessor. Of course the "Eddie Haskel characters" grabbed onto the new commander with the now familiar suck ups of "gee, sir, it's so great to finally have a real commander, you're so much better than your predecessor, etc." I was surprised and disappointed that one of my fellow company commanders was quick to abandon someone who had clearly been mistreated. I asked this company commander why he was now openly ridiculing the old commander and he gave me some rubbish about the commander not supporting him on some insignificant issue regarding training. "What bullshit," I told him.

Nonetheless, we had a new battalion commander and we immediately had a five-day training exercise to allow him to size up the unit and identify the deadwood. Shortly before dark on the second day we gathered in the operations tent and received an operations order for the battalion to execute a night move to a new location. After the orders had been presented the battalion commander asked if there were any questions. I said, "This is not a question but a clarification, given the bad weather, I have three OH58s that will wait and move in the morning. These are new pilots that don't have the experience to fly tonight."

Then things got really crazy when the battalion commander jumped out of his chair and barked, "Get up front and stand at attention." My first thought was "Oh crap, here we go again."

"What do you mean they can't fly tonight?" the commander demanded. I responded "Sir, these three pilots are right out of Flight School, they have less than twenty hours in the OH-58 and the weather is marginal. They aren't prepared to fly single pilot, in this weather and at night." The commander was indignant "I won't have pilots that can't fly. You send them up or I want you to take their wings," he told me. I responded with the only thing I could say, "Sir, these are not bad pilots, they are just inexperienced. As their commander I have to make sure these pilots aren't put in a situation they aren't prepared for. This is clearly the situation tonight." The commander was done talking and said, "I told you what to do. No more discussion." Some people in attendance resented that I had been given command in the first place so for them there was a hopeful expectation that I would be fired on the spot. I had some friends in the room but in this command environment I didn't want any of them to become collateral damage to myself.

I returned to my company and gave my plan for the night move. I left the three OH-58 pilots in place until morning and moved the rest of my company that night. When we met in operations the next day, there was no mention of my decision to leave the three pilots and no further discussion about taking their wings.

By this time in my career I had adopted what I called the "Sixty-Minute Test." I would explain this to my junior officers like this: "Imagine that this decision or action somehow blows up and you find yourself on the CBS 60 Minutes Program and you have fifteen seconds to explain what you did and why. Ask yourself if you can explain that you acted first, in the best interest of the Army; second, in the best interest of your troops; and third, not simply in your personal best interest. If you can't pass this test then stop what you are about to do and don't do it." Putting my pilots up that night would not pass this test.

Was this the worse leader I would fall victim to? Yes, in the Army this is the great sin, this is absolutely the worse thing a commander can do. Against the overwhelming facts not to do this, he was willing to put pilots in danger simply for him to make a personal splash. I will experience personal betrayal by senior leaders later in my career but this was the greatest sin I would see in my career.

About six months later, one of the companies in our Battalion had a terrible crash and the four-man crew were all killed. The accident investigation report published by the US Army Safety Center identified several points of failure by the company commander that directly contributed to the crash. I understood why that company commander made the fateful choices and launched that flight. But I fear that if I had succumbed to the pressure and made those bad decisions, I would never be able to outlive the guilt I would feel.

To summarize the lessons from this "If They Can't Fly I Want Their Wings" adventure. First, I was absolutely on the brink of being fired on the spot. Relief from command means end of career. I would linger for a year or two but I would be flushed out in shame. But frankly that probability did not enter my evaluation process. I knew the right answer and no one was going to coerce me into doing what I knew to be wrong.

Second, dangerous situations are not limited to the Army. In industry you have the daily pressures of meeting schedules and cost objectives. Under those pressures decisions are made every day that put employees at risk such as putting drivers behind the wheel of vehicles and operators at the controls of heavy equipment, work environments with the exposure to high voltage and dangerous chemicals, shop environments with dangerous machines, construction environments with the dangers of falling and being crushed, and bad weather with fog, snow, and ice.

Third, for the first time, I had to rethink my understanding of the Army and its values. In my previous assignments, I simply had the bad luck with getting bad battalion commanders as I finished my tours. Despite those bad experiences I was still embracing the "duty, honor, country" ethos I had learned as a second lieutenant in Berlin. But now I saw how an entire brigade could slip into a toxic command environment. I had seen three battalion commanders have their careers trashed by an angry hurt old man. Then I saw the new replacement commanders who were so afraid of suffering the same fate they acted in totally unacceptable ways. The new ethos was "I will do whatever is necessary to protect my career." After advising my peers to not give up on the Army because of one bad commander, I was wondering if I was a fool and that the true character of the Army was far less than what I romanticized it to be.

CHAPTER 9

Just Sign the Inventory

As an Aviation captain I was privileged to command two separate companies in the prototype Division Aviation Brigade (Air Attack). Prior to assuming the first command, I attended the division's in-house Company Commander's Pre-Command Course. During this course I learned a critical lesson from the Assistant Division Commander (Brigadier General). His advice went like this "as a commander you will be juggling many things and will sometime feel you are under pressure—you will face a problem and think, "If I just take a shortcut. This problem will go away and I can move to the next problem. When that happens you need to stop, you need to remember that there are no shortcuts, shortcuts will lead to bigger problems downstream. Do the right thing every time, regardless of the immediate negative consequences."

Jump forward eighteen months and I'm a captain commanding my second company, a 22-ship, 150-man Aviation company. When you take command of a company, you inventory and sign for every piece of property and equipment in the unit; helicopters, vehicles, weapons, tools, bunk beds, sheets, desks, spare parts, etc. When you leave and turn the company over to the next commander, he does an inventory and you are personally responsible for anything that has gone missing and you must pay for it. I remember my brigade commander joking that "every command costs you at least one month's pay at your change of command inventory." The Division Supply Regulation dictated that Change of Command Efficiency Reports for any commander who couldn't account for all his property would include the statement "This commander could not perform property accountability." Ouch, that's a career killer, which is why outgoing commanders are willing to pay large amounts for lost equipment. You never lost big things like jeeps or night vision goggles but the little things like tools and sheets can quickly add up to thousands of dollars. One Aviation maintenance officer in a sister company who, after signing for the equipment in the hanger, carried her hand receipt with her for three months because the financial liability was crushing her.

For the point of this story, between the motor pool, hanger, Aviation mechanics, motor pool mechanics, and arms room, I had over twenty thousand hand tools. Our Division Supply Office had a process for sending a "10 percent inventory" to each company every month with a list of items to inventory. The idea was this would help the company commander because over the course of twelve months you would inventory your entire company. The requirement was for the company commander to personally perform the inventory and execute the financial recovery for any missing items and have them placed on order. When you signed the Divisions Monthly Inventory you were certifying that not only was the inventory done but that the final financial actions had taken place and replacement items placed on order. This was not a bad idea and under some circumstances this would assist the company commander with property accountability. But it was an idea probably better suited for the Division Finance Company then an extremely large unit with extended field requirements like mine. Or it could be argued that large companies like mine would benefit the most and of course, division headquarters is there to help you.

Yah, right, let's talk about that for a minute. This was 1980 and I had just attended what was an early "Computer Expo" in Seattle and saw the new Apple III and how it could be used for of all things, inventory management. I'm not an intuitive person but I sent a short paper to the division headquarters with an explanation of how I thought these Apple III computers could be used to automate the tool inventory records at large companies such as mine. I received a very direct answer that I could not misunderstand, "Computers are not needed in company supply rooms. If Captain Hancock can't do tool control he should not be a company commander." Okay, thank you very much for considering my idea. That will teach me to keep my good ideas to myself, and apparently, I will never have to worry about learning how to use a computer.

But back to the story. Our brigade had just started the five-month Department of the Army Directed Force Modernization Evaluation. Our training rotation was to deploy to a training area 250 miles away for four weeks of maneuvers, then return to garrison for one week and then back to the training area to repeat the rotation three more times. During our week in garrison we continued to provide daily support to the division so we were still working ten-hour days but got to sleep at home in a bed. Predictably in the middle of the second field exercise I received a notice to inventory all of my tools.

My first action was to send a written request to our Battalion Supply Officer (S-4) asking for technical assistance with completing the inventory primarily because I had no supply sergeant. My request was denied with a formal memo, which he presented personally with a big smile which essentially said, "Eat shit and die because I'm not doing your job for you, if you can't inventory your tools you shouldn't be a company commander." Okay, sometimes a no is as good as a yes, because now I know to look for help elsewhere.

So I met with the battalion commander and laid out my problem and asked that he endorse a request to division that this particular inventory be postponed until after our evaluation was complete. I fully expected his support but the discussion went like this, "Sir, I've received a 10 percent inventory for all of my tools. I need to get it postponed until after this evaluation is over. I've prepared a request to division supply laying out our field requirements and my staffing shortfall and asking that the inventory be postponed until the evaluation is over. Will you endorse it?" The battalion commander answered, "No."

"Unbelievable," I thought but I had no choice but to continue forward so I said, "Sir, you know my situation in the supply room. I need your help with this." The commander was angry and said, "Just sign the damn inventory and get Division off your back, I'm not getting involved in this."

"Thank you for your time, sir," I said and left.

So I sent my request directly to the division supply office without going through my battalion headquarters. This was a breach of protocol, but I felt I had to proceed on my own. I received a speedy response from Division, which was simply "Request denied, send your completed inventory within one week." So I put the inventory requirement away and focused on the readiness of my unit and the next tactical evaluation. Two weeks later I received a letter from the Division Supply Officer directing me to report to his office when I was next in garrison.

Immediately upon my return, I reported to the Division Supply Officer. He was a lieutenant colonel and we had one of the most remarkable meetings of my career. It started out a little edgy when the LTC started the meeting by asking me, "Captain, why do you refuse to do this inventory?"

I responded "Sir, I tried to lay it out in my request for postponement. Basically I have no supply sergeant, I have twenty thousand tools, the tools are in three different geographic locations, and I'm in the middle of a five-month Department of the Army Directed Force Modernization Evaluation being conducted 250 miles away and the requirement is that I personally inventory each tool, recovery money for any loses and order replacement items. Bottom line is I simply can't do it."

The LTC said, "Why didn't you ask for help from your Battalion S-4?" I responded by handing him my original request for help and the "eat, shit, and die" memo that the S-4 had given me. "Oh," the LTC said, "then why didn't you ask for help from your battalion commander?" I responded with "Sir, I did ask for help and he told me to simply sign the inventory and pretend that I did it."

Now for the really good part. The LTC said to me, "Captain, you've been F——ed." My response was "Thank you, sir, you're the first son of a bitch that agrees with me." At that point the LTC relaxed and sat back in his chair and said, "You are right not to sign the inventory if you haven't personally done it." I responded with great relief "thank you, sir."

"So what am I to do with you?" he asked.

"Your next inventory is your 82 Camouflage Net Sets with components (1,500 items). Can you do this?"

"Yes, sir," I told him. "Good. I will approve your original request canceling the tools inventory and it will come up again in twelve months when your tactical evaluation is complete. My response will go through your battalion commander so you can expect some heat but remember, you did the right thing here, you never sign for something you haven't done," he told me.

"Thank you, sir," I told him with all gratitude.

When the approval arrived at the battalion, I was called to a meeting with my battalion commander who had the S-4 with him. They were both very angry and it was clear that had spent some time getting each other worked up. "What's the problem?" I asked. "The Division Supply Staff aren't a bunch of bureaucrats, they looked at my circumstances and made a reasoned decision to support me."

Seven months later, I turned the company over to my replacement. It had taken a lot of work but the change of command inventory was perfect, everything was accounted for. The monthly inventories generated by Division Supply were a good tool but my success in this case was due to the equipment accountability disciplines I developed in the motor pool in Korea.

At the beginning of this story I told you about a brigadier general who warned me about taking the easy/expedient/wrong way to handle a problem. This inventory problem is exactly what he was warning about. This wasn't a combat situation were victory or defeat or life or death demanded ingenuity and thinking outside the box. This was simply a peace time bureaucratic requirement that required it be given the priority it deserved.

About 1990, I attended a "Quality Systems" seminar conducted by the late W. Edwards Deming. He had an audience participation exercise he called "The Red Bead Experiment." This has been copied by many management instructors but they primarily use it illustrate variation in processes. In the Deming presentation he focused equally on variation but also on the psychological aspects of the workforce. He illustrated how when people feel boxed in by systems and processes that they can't control, they will cheat and lie to protect their jobs. This of course was the situation my battalion commander presented me with when he said "just sign the damn inventory and get Division off your back, I'm not getting involved in this."

In industry you can frequently be told to do something that appears to fix a problem. When you are told to charge your time or expenses to the wrong charge code, what do you do? If you are charging your time on a government contract this could result in criminal prosecution for fraud. There was a recent episode with health care workers at the Veterans Administration falsifying patient wait time records because it was out of their control and they wanted to protect their jobs. Mr. Deming was exactly correct.

Was this the worse leader I would fall victim to? This is the same commander from my earlier, "If They Can't Fly I want Their Wings" adventure so yes he was. But, this inventory problem was not a great sin. It was simply another example of his terribly bad leadership.

To summarize the lessons from this "Just Sign the Inventory" adventure: First, take the general's advice to heart and when you are pressured to take a shortcut step back and do the right thing. I never saw this general again while I was in that Division. But I ran into him several years later and I told him about this important advice and that it had served me very well as a company commander. It continues to serve me well these many years later and it always will.

Second, never claim to have done something you haven't. Standup and take the admonishment and whatever consequences follow.

Third, if you claim to have done something that you have not done, expect that it will be revealed. To be revealed as a liar, is something you will never recover from. You can never do something alone in a vacuum. Someone knows you have lied and it will undermine your credibility on other matters. Ben Franklin said it best "three people can keep a secret if two of them are dead."

Fourth, when you are in leadership, you are responsible to provide the tools and processes that allow you employees to succeed. When you don't do this, you can expect your employees to do whatever is required to protect themselves even if it means lying and cheating.

Fifth, sometimes people refuse to do their jobs and you have to find ways to overcome them. The Battalion S-4 and battalion commander in this story are not unique. I faced countless situations that were similar to this one. After leaving the Army a friend confided in me that "you are reluctant to ask people for help." Yes, I know his assessment was correct. I think that through situations like this inventory problem I try to avoid leaving myself vulnerable to people. I think I'm better off to make my own best arrangements than to have a request for help thrown back in my face.

CHAPTER 10

You're Not Helping Me!

The year is 1983. I'm still a captain and I've rotated out of my Infantry division. Despite my best efforts to be assigned elsewhere, I'm doing my obligatory assignment in the Training and Doctrine Command (TRADOC) at Ft. Rucker, the Army Aviation Center. I asked Washington to assign me to a couple of active flying assignments but in the end, I was assigned to Ft. Rucker. At that time the Army Training and Doctrine Command was organized around the Army's thirteen branches and each had a school house: Ft. Benning for Infantry, Ft. Sill for Artillery, Ft. Eustis for Transportation, etc. Each school house was organized in the template which was named School Model 76, which generally meant that each school had a Director of Combat Development (DOCD), Director of Training Developments (DOTD), etc.

Each of these Directorates was led by a full colonel. Post Headquarters had a "Command Group" with at least two General Officers and a Chief of Staff who was a full colonel. There were other "Tenant Organizations" that had an Aviation related mission but who reported to people elsewhere like the Army Research Lab (ARL) so they were politely tolerated but were never part of the Ft. Rucker "inner circle."

The "inner circle" at Ft. Rucker consisted of the Post Headquarters and this group of ten or so directors. Most of the "directors" were old-time Aviation insiders who were camped out finishing their careers. These directors were preoccupied with undercutting each other and jockeying for the privilege of sitting next to the general at lunch. Since I was only a captain none of this soap opera activity interested me but it frequently did affect me. I had several misadventures which I will write about in a follow-on book if I survive writing this one.

Shortly after my arrive at Ft. Rucker the Army established Aviation as a new "Branch" the same as Infantry, Field Artillery, Armor, etc. I received a letter from Washington notifying me that I was moved from Infantry to Aviation. I immediately called Washington and objected that I hadn't asked to be moved and wanted to remain in the Infantry. After he stopped laughing, my branch control officer told me that I owed the Army two more years in Aviation as a condition of my going to Flight School and that I could call back then if I still wanted to change to Infantry. I was really disappointed because my plan of being the dual Infantry/Aviator was now trashed. I had never considered being anything but an infantryman and I'm sure that if I had foreseen this happening back in Berlin, that I would not have applied for Flight School. But this decision was out of my control and at least I was still a "Combat Arms Officer" so I put my head down and embrace my new identity as an Aviation officer.

When the Army does a reorganization, there are organizational winners and losers. At Ft. Rucker we established an "Aviation Proponancy Office" to bring in missions we thought belong with Aviation. Of course these missions belonged to other organizations so they understandably circled their wagons attempting to protect their mission and budget dollars. Perhaps the classic dog fight was with Ft. Benning over Air Assault Proponancy. The question was simple, if Ft. Benning is the proponent for Airborne Doctrine and Training (parachuting), who owns Air Assault Doctrine and Training (helicopters)? Predictably, both Ft. Benning and Ft. Rucker claimed the prize. Another dog fight was over who should own Aviation Logistics—Ft. Rucker or Ft. Eustis? And at Army Level, does the Chief of Aviation have an equal voice with the Chief of Infantry?

You can imagine the excitement our directors felt as they found themselves in key positions to establish their legacies as the first "Princes in the new Royalty of Aviation Branch." Now there would be funding for an "Aviation Branch Museum" and who would have their photo hanging there? We got the remarkably inexpensive but highly coveted "Aviation Branch Coin." My coin is in a box in my attic waiting to be discovered and discarded by my children after I'm dead. The coins were serial numbered and the first coin number "One" was purchased by a good friend of mine who was assigned at Ft. Rucker but was not an Aviator. He was an Artillery officer and assigned to Ft. Rucker in his secondary specialty in the Comptroller's Office. His number "One" coin is on proud display in his home office. To close out this discussion on the Aviation Branch Coin, for a short time I managed a subordinate captain who's highlight for his entire three-year tour at Ft. Rucker was that he had been on the committee that designed the "Aviation Branch Coin." He left disappointed that this monumental (in reality inconsequential) contribution to Aviation Branch was not adequately acknowledged and rewarded.

Organizational structures are never stable and are always under stress as different factions try to take mission and budget from the others. This is no different in the commercial world. Who is driving the corporate train: Engineering? Production? Quality? Who takes the brunt of budget cuts? What is the background of the new president and where do his priorities lay? Fundamentally and very naturally, the first question anyone thinks about in this situation is "How does this affect me and my future."

As I started my last year at Ft. Rucker, a new colonel arrived and was appointed as our director. "The director" was my senior rater and this played out as another repeat of suffering under a poor leader for the end of my tour. But for the director, instead of being the crowning glory of his career, this assignment was his worst nightmare. He immediately found himself in the outer fringe of the directors and of course he resented it. The harder he tried to get into the inner circle the more he was marginalized. He really had no chance of making a splash because after all, some of these directors had been in their positions for years and were skilled at laying traps for the new guys.

It's unfortunate to see anyone who has their feelings hurt in this way and it puts your teeth on edge when you see the things they do in foolish attempts to be recognized. Back when I was in Germany we had a lieutenant who led morning physical training with a bayonet in his teeth. He did this in an attempt to be recognized as a hard ass and be elevated above his peers. This backfired badly and he quickly became the poster child for a weak adolescent lieutenant. His stunt earned him a dubious spot in the leadership curriculum at the Infantry School as an example of bad leadership mistakes. Like that twenty-two-year-old lieutenant, our forty-seven-year-old colonel was desperate to somehow distinguish himself with the general and like that lieutenant he made a major mistake.

Initially I got along fine with this new director and I enjoyed a position of trust and responsibility. We had a very weak LTC above me and the director would take major projects away from the LTC and assign them to me. This LTC was kind of like the ghost officers I wrote about in chapter 2: "I'm Too Smart To Be an Infantryman." This was grueling for me but when you are willing to work sixty hours a week and have good organization skills you can get a lot done.

But our good relationship didn't last long and the first chink in our relationship was probably my fault. The Army was trying to formalize the "mentorship program." The idea was that a senior officer would develop a formal "mentor/mentee" relationship with a junior officer and find ways to advise and guide that junior officer's career which included influencing his assignments and schooling. You can see that this could easily become a "sugar daddy" relationship and captains were scheming to hook up with influential senior officers. Naturally this mentor/mentee would be a tight personal relationship.

So one day, the director asked me what I thought of him being my mentor. I'm not intuitive but I realized this was a dangerous situation. I had seen the dark side of this new director, which I will discuss momentarily and knew it would be a mistake to be tied up in a relationship with him. I was on the spot to give an answer so I responded, "Thank you, sir, that's very generous, let me think about it and get back to you." Ouch! He raised his eyebrow as he understood this was a nice way of saying no. "If he doesn't say yes, then he's saying no" is an old axiom. So this ended a positive relationship but I knew that if you have this type of tight relationship with someone you are morally/ethically incompatible with, that you have made a deal with the devil and it will be a disaster.

The dark side I had seen with this director centered on an "intern" working in my group. The intern program was a three-year program where the intern would receive an assortment of formal training and work experience with the end goal that he could perform "operations analyst" functions similar to what the captains in my group were performing. Shortly after his arrival, the director had me into his office and told me to "get rid" of the intern and bring in someone else. I explained the intern program and showed the satisfactory performance appraisal from the intern's first year and reported that the intern was developing just fine and there were no performance issues to justify taking any adverse action. The director simply looked at me and said "I told you, I want him out of here." The problem for the director was that the intern was a retired Army noncommissioned officer about the same age as the director and also that he was a black man.

I saw the danger to my intern and did two things; first I made certain that the intern's training records were complete, airtight, and any audit would substantiate that he was performing satisfactorily. Second, I realized that I was leaving a few months before his two-year performance appraisal would be done so I wrote an interim appraisal documenting his year up to the point of my departure. The official appraisal system didn't accommodate an "interim report" so my appraisal was in the form of a personal

"Letter of Commendation" to the intern for his contributions to the organization, documenting his accomplishments, expressing my expectation that he would have no difficulty completing the full program and would enjoy a long government civilian career. This was not anecdotal fluff; it was genuine, substantive and factual. When I gave the letter to him I cautioned him that with me leaving, we could expect some changes and that he should keep this close by in case there be any confusion on his performance up to now.

To close this part of the story, a few months after my departure I received a call from one of my captain's back at Ft. Rucker. He relayed that when I left, the director took ownership of the intern's program and when he did the annual appraisal he had the intern in and told him his performance was unsatisfactory and he was being terminated. The intern calmly responded that he was confused and gave him a copy of my "Letter of Commendation." Check mate and game over. My intern was safe. As I said, I'm not an intuitive person but it was the director's first instruction to torpedo my intern that told me not to become entangled in the mentor relationship with him.

In the midst of the Branch turf war, the director thought he saw an opportunity to scarf up some mission from another branch and present it to our general as a gift. He authored a paper arguing that OV-1 Mohawk Systems Training should be taken away from the Military Intelligence School at Ft.

Huachuca and moved to Ft Rucker. I learned that the plan was hatched at Happy Hour one night when the director met a couple of Warrant Officer Instructor Pilots from the OV-1 Qualification Course who told him the OV-1 Systems Training should be moved to Ft. Rucker. Without talking to anyone, he drafted a position paper that argued the mission should move to Ft. Rucker and took it to the general who signed it and sent it to TRADOC Headquarters.

Our director enjoyed about three weeks as the general's confidant on this issue before the roof fell in on him. The Intelligence School sent in their rebuttal listing twenty years of analysis and three separate studies, which validated why that mission belonged at their school. Our director found himself in a tough spot because he hadn't done any analysis and had simply parroted anecdotal arguments fed to him by some warrant officers he was buying drinks for. "Bring us another round and we will tell you another story." It is an old joke that someone acting impulsively and not doing due diligence is guilty of "ready, shoot, aim" and that was clearly the case here. Oh my goodness, how desperate was he?

This became personal when I was called to the director's office and was told to fix the problem. He had sent our weak LTC out to the Intelligence School to strike an agreement and they rejected him so now he threw the problem to me. This first thing I learned was that his two Warrant Officer—Subject Matter Experts had both retired a few weeks after he met them and he stepped out on this limb. The second thing I learned was that TRADOC Headquarters was 100 percent aligned with the Intelligence School. His position paper was simply old anecdotal arguments which had been raised and dismissed repeatedly in the past. They were good for happy hour banter but not for Army Mission Realignment.

I gave my report to this tortured man and it was not received well. The director put the blame on me by saying, "You aren't helping me!" My response was, "Sir, this has all been wrung out several times. I don't know what else I can do." The director was frantic. "You have to think of new arguments. You have to think of better arguments. You have until tomorrow to come up with something."

I responded, "I will try my best but I have to tell you I don't know that I will have anything new." The director said, "You and your group will stay here in the office and not go home until you think of something new."

"I don't know what you mean," I offered up. The director assumed his most authoritative posture and said, "Your group is not to go home until I release you. I have a dinner engagement tonight, and I will call afterward for you to report your progress." I could only have one response, "Yes, sir, I understand for myself and the other officers but what about my civilian secretary."

He spat out, "No one goes home until I release you, do you understand, Captain?"

"The only thing missing here is that I'm not standing at attention," I thought.

I asked my secretary if she could stay late and I was relieved when she said with a big smile, "Captain, I wouldn't miss this for the world." Our wives brought us dinner and we gave it a good try but we couldn't come up with any new arguments. At 10:00 PM, I hadn't heard from the director so I sent everyone home. They all offered to stay longer, but I had a responsibility to treat them with respect. I hung out another half hour and then went home myself. As you have already guessed, in the end I had nothing new to offer.

The general was upset that he had been misled and embarrassed by this failed mission grab. I'm sure he could hear the staff at the Intelligence School laughing from 1,400 miles away. The director blamed his staff for not supporting him. The Command Group marginalized him further and all he was allowed to do was schedule the classrooms. Instead of sitting next to the general at lunch, he was assigned to the kids' table.

I was offered an opportunity for reconciliation before I was reassigned and left Ft. Rucker. Unable to stick his head outside of our building, the director formed an Investment Club. For $2,000 any of us could join his club and learn about investing in the stock market. I'm not sure exactly how the portfolios worked but the important part was that you had a standing club meeting from ten to eleven each morning in the director's office and he would call the broker on the speaker phone and they would discuss how the investments were doing and other strategies. The weak LTC was one of the first members and recommended that this would be a good investment in my career because I would be getting an efficiency report in a few months. He may have been correct about this but like the "Mentor Program" my instincts told me to run away from this as fast as I could. So I told him thanks and that I would think about it but I had already decided to pass on the Investment Club and take my chances on the efficiency report.

This was about my eleventh year of active duty and happily I came out on the promotion list to major. I was also approaching the window for reassignment so now that I knew I was being promoted, I had to figure out where I wanted to be assigned next and get out ahead of my assignments officer. This is where an influential mentor could steer you into a good assignment or graduate school. As a major it made no sense to try to go back to the Infantry because I had not commanded an Infantry Company. If Infantry was willing to take me, I wouldn't be competitive for promotion to LTC. In Washington, Officer Records was managing me as an Aviation Operations Officer. The really fun things like parachuting and flying Cobra Gunships were behind me and the likely assignments were Recruiting Command, Reserve Officer Training Corp (ROTC) and Reserve Component Advisor. These are all important parts of the Army and would have all been good assignments.

But frankly, the luster of being a Combat Arms Officer and the ethos of "duty, honor, country" were wearing thin as the reality of the Army was finally sinking in. Despite the tremendous emotional highs that I experienced and still treasure, and although I worked for some of the finest men I have never known, and although I led troops in very excellent units, I had to face the reality that most of my senior leaders were terrible people and I had been miserable working under them. "How do I attract these rat bastards? What's wrong with me? If these guys represent success, is this really what I want?" These were all questions that troubled me greatly.

About this time, I became aware that Washington had a small group of officers assigned to work in Contracting, Acquisition, and Weapons Systems Program Management. A few years later this became the Acquisition Corps. I saw this as an opportunity to learn the business side of the Army.

I liked so many parts of the Army culture. For example I liked simply wearing the uniform, everyone knowing what the food chain is, going to a meeting and everyone knows who's in charge and even where to sit. But in many ways, the Army is a little fantasy world and at some point the Army spits you out and you have to understand contractual relationships and how to work with regular people. "I'm the colonel and you're the captain" simply doesn't work well anywhere except the Army. By working in contracting, I saw the opportunity to learn these lessons while still on active duty.

But I needed advice, so I sought out a director that I did not know personally and had never even spoken with. I first heard him speak when I graduated from the Cobra Qualification Course and he was the commander of Attack Helicopter Training Branch. I remember thinking, "If I were the commander that is exactly what I would tell this group." After that, I had watched him for two years and found him unique among the directors. First of all, he was not involved in the petty back biting and maneuvering of the power structure that I spoke about earlier. Watching him it was clear that he was secure with himself and understood his priorities were to be a good Christian, a good husband and father, and a good soldier. I asked for an appointment, and we had a very frank and open discussion. After talking with him I made the decision to change from Aviation Operations to Aviation Acquisition. I never worked for this colonel so it's unusual that we formed this relationship. But I'm certain that God put him in my life at this point and he continued to be a trusted advisor for the next forty years and I regret to report that he was buried at Arlington National Cemetery in October 2016. He is one of the four finest men I have ever known.

My relationship with my director continued to deteriorate. When he learned that I had changed to Aviation Acquisition he was upset and told me "it is selfish and unprofessional, your setting yourself up for work after the Army." Behind his animosity, I understood that he would soon be forced out of the Army and had no prospects for work on the outside. To him my change from Operations to Acquisition also meant "you don't want to be like me when you grow up." After this tongue lashing, he quit talking to me. I was not alone as totally unrelated to me; he also stopped talking with his LTC deputy.

A few weeks later, my phone was ringing off the hook with calls from friends around the country. "Do Canadians still speak French and the list for the Command and General Staff College was released last night, congratulations you're on it." Like a promotion, selection to this school was made by a board of officers in Washington and this was a very important event. I sat at my desk Thursday and Friday waiting for my director to call or come by and congratulate me. He was silent. In the Army, this is a sever breach of protocol and although I'm not an intuitive person, I knew this an unmistakable statement that he had written me off.

Two months before I left Ft. Rucker, my promotion number came up and this meant we would have a promotion ceremony at Ft. Rucker and not at the Command and General Staff College. Protocol dictated that my director be the person to promote me and you can see how terribly awkward this was for both of us. Some well-connected captains might ask the general to promote them but I was not connected in this way so it never entered my mind. Frankly I didn't care who promoted me but I knew I could express no preference other than my director. "Of course, I hope the director will be the one promoting me," I would say to anyone who asked.

My promotion gave the director a couple of problems, first he knew everyone on the base expected him to be the one to promote his subordinates. On this point he was firm that no, he did not want to pass this to anyone, it was his moment and he wasn't going to let anyone else do it. The other obvious problem was that he didn't like me and everyone in our directorate knew it. All things considered he would rather have me out of the Army and not moving up the ranks so how was this going to play out?

The standard promotion ceremony requires the director to give the standard promotion speech, which includes commending me on my performance, talking about my great family, talking about my lovely and supportive wife, talking about my potential for a long career and talking about my future contributions to the Army. "Damn, no crap," I could see him saying. Happily, the director rose to the occasion and gave a brief but gracious speech that was most acceptable. For my part, I was equally gracious and talked about what a wonderful career the Army had provided me and how I was grateful for the help of my coworkers. Anyone on the outside watching this would say, "How nice, what a wonderful ceremony, what a delicious cake and lots of it too." To everyone in the room it was simply an affirmation that the director would play his part and not embarrass me in this public forum. What a joke, here I was at what should have been a great moment in my career but instead I was playing out a delicate dance with a dangerous adversary who could not wait to torpedo me.

Was this the worse leader I would fall victim to? No, he was difficult to work for but he never committed the great sin of a commander. I had experienced the great sin and will experience blatant betrayal be senior officers again but this director was guilty of neither. If the nature of our work had been different and had physical danger, I suspect that he very well could have committed the great sin but we were just doing office work.

To summarize the lessons from this "You're Not Helping Me!" adventure. First, it was a heartbreaking emotional struggle to give up my basic career goal of staying thirty years and being a battalion commander. I had always viewed commanding as the only worthwhile or purposeful job in the Army. But at this point, I had experienced so many bad senior officers that I had to ask myself "is this the only way to define success and can I even take another twenty years of this?" More importantly I asked, "What is God doing with me? What am I supposed to be learning from this repeating cycle of bad leaders." Through this process, I reached the decision that if I could survive a total of twenty years that it would be enough and I would get out.

Second, similar to my first assignment as a second lieutenant supporting an Ordnance depot, I didn't want to be assigned at Ft. Rucker. But in hindsight I'm sure it was the right assignment for me at that time. Primarily it was a time for me to develop staffing and writing skills and to spend time at home with my family without the extended field duty of my previous assignments.

Third, everyone needs to feel he has a contribution to make and that he brings value to the organization. This is true from the newest private to the most senior officers. It is a fundamental responsibility of leaders to provide an environment where everyone is treated with respect for themselves as individuals and for the work they do. I would go to great effort in the future to make sure that no one under my control felt marginalized.

Fourth, when people feel they need to do something to fight back or to distinguish themselves, their judgment usually fails them and they make a mess of things. I witnessed how this need caused my director/colonel to act like a new second lieutenant.

Fifth, how you respond to rejection is 100 percent under your control. When it happens to you, it hurts a great deal, no it hurts tremendously. But you can't make people love you and it's foolish to try. You have to do your best to not let your pain turn into bitterness or let it poison your other relationships. I discussed my problems with my wife and she was a good sounding board. I can't imagine how this colonel's pain was played out at home with his family, but I fear it was not good.

Sixth, you have to be selective in your relationships and cautious to not become entangled with people who you are ethically or morally incompatible with. I chose to not get entangled with my director and it cost me professionally but in the midst of it I was lucky to find a senior officer to give me advise. I sought him out because I watched him and judged him to be a man of integrity and competence. I have learned many times that God places people in your life when you need them and they help you get through your problems.

CHAPTER 11

You Need a Defense Attorney

Background: I'm now a major assigned as a Contracting Officer buying Aviation Systems. I have a contracting officer's "Warrant," which authorized me to sign contracts and commit the government. I worked under the direction of a GS-15 division chief but my rater is a member of the Senior Executive Service (SES), which is a government civilian who holds the grade equal to a general officer and my senior rater is a brigadier general. You will see that this rating scheme worked out to be critical as this story unfolds.

I have to say that I had a lot of trouble writing this last story. It's just too complex. There are too many details, too many regulatory and legal nuances, too many players and it covered over three years. So I thought I would leave it out. But I realized that if I was writing about how God had his hand in keeping me safe and securing my career, then I simply can't leave it out.

The short story about being a government contracting officer is that it is centered on having a "Warrant." A "Warrant" allows you to sign contracts and commit the government on business matters. To receive a "Warrant" and perform as a contracting officer you have to complete a number of training courses (Contracting, Business Law, Cost/Pricing Analysis, etc.) and a have a variety of contracting experience (Production, Research and Development, Services, etc.). When I met these requirements, my "Warrant" was awarded to me in a small ceremony by my SES. Contracting turned out to be good fit for me.

I enjoyed working with Contract Law and performing the analysis required to form a good contract. Army contracts are governed by the Federal Acquisition Regulation (FAR) which provides the framework for the analysis and ensures that all actions are reviewed as necessary by the local acquisition policy, legal, pricing, engineering, production control, etc. It establishes broad requirements but cannot account for every possible contingency that will come up so you have to have some level of "business acumen." Those that don't have the acumen can't be trusted to be a buyer and are moved into areas like policy, production, and liaison.

After I had managed several large Engineering Development Contracts including the APACHE Stinger Missile Integration and APACHE Airborne Target Handoff System Integration, my SES asked me to take on a special project. This special project was to resolve a large group of advisory audits conducted by a couple of audit agencies, which advised that the government may have been overcharged by one of our helicopter suppliers. There were about thirty-five audits dating back several years and he wanted me to try to figure them out and close them. In simple terms my job was to research each audit, determine if the Army was over charged, to collect any funds due, dismiss any audit findings that were unsubstantiated, and close each audit.

I initially had trouble obtaining cooperation from the helicopter company. I started the project with a $2 million audit. The company sent a letter stating that they simply rejected that the government had a legal right to investigate their pricing and they would not participate. I reviewed this with my SES and requested that I be allowed to execute a "Final Decision" on the audit and unilaterally reduce their contract by $2 million. He was hesitant because this is obviously the nuclear option and represents a total brake down in a business relationship. But since they had written a letter clearly stating that they would not cooperate, he agreed to support my request. The $2 million reduction provided a new spirit of cooperation by the helicopter company and my SES personally worked with the President of the company and secured their cooperation and provided a coordinated schedule for audit review and closure.

It took several months, but I completed my analysis of all thirty-five audits and I was ready to negotiate settlements. In general, I found that most of the audits had no basis and we had no claim to a refund. I documented the details of my findings and staffed my results through policy, cost analysis, legal, etc. I received a non-concurrence from our legal department. They didn't identify any mistakes in my work; they simply didn't know what to do and didn't want to move forward. I reported to my SES that my work was complete but that I was blocked from proceeding because of the legal non-concurrence.

Within a few days my SES, GS-15 division chief and myself were called to the general's office and asked why I was stalled on settling and closing the audits. My SES was terrific as he explained the work I had done and the problem we had with the legal review. He walked the general through the regulatory and legal requirements and recommended that the general exercise his regulatory authority and close the audits. After considering this, the general directed me personally, to proceed despite the legal non-concurrence. He looked me in the eye and instructed me, "Major, I'm directing you to close these audits immediately." As you read in my earlier adventures of "If They Can't Fly I want Their Wings," "Just Sign the Inventory," and "You're not Helping Me," I don't simply jump and do what my leaders direct me to. So for this story it's absolutely critical to tell you that this was a lawful order and the Federal Acquisition Regulation and all Federal Contract Law gave the general authority to give this direction. The next day my SES gave me his hand written instructions to proceed and execute the settlement. The word "execute" the settlement is a critical word in contracting as it is means only one thing which is to "sign the document." These handwritten instructions would be very important to me later.

With the help of my GS-15 division chief, I negotiated the settlement of these audits and gave directions to the company for recovery of the funds the government was owed. The project then moved to the recovery phase.

Unrelated to this project, Washington moved me to a different organization and the recovery phase of my settlement was passed to a different government civilian contracting officer. This move was not related to my contracting project but was an important move into a position of higher complexity in a different arena of weapons system acquisition management. Since I changed organizations I received an Officer Efficiency Report (OER) in which my SES and general each wrote the highest praise for my "exceptional work" on closing this project. In a strange twist of fate, that you will see momentarily, the general had previously not been my senior rater but inserted himself over my objection. That was the last OER to go into my records prior to the Lieutenant Colonel Promotion Board and I was certain that it helped me to be promoted in a year that the selection rate was only 50 percent. A few months after of my departure, my SES retired and the general was promoted.

Within a year, I was called to the Department of Defense Inspector General's Office (DoDIG) in Washington, DC, and asked to explain how this settlement had come about. I asked what prompted their interest and they told me that someone had asked them to look into it because they thought it was unusual. It took several hours and I laid it out in excruciating detail explaining: the who, the what, the when, the why, etc., of the entire project. To my surprise they were openly outraged that the general had directed me to proceed in the face of a legal non-concurrence. I walked them through the regulations and explained why the general had the authority to do this and recommended that they should speak with the general to confirm my explanation. When I left, they were very unhappy because to them, being lawyers themselves, they could think of no circumstances that the general would move forward when the lawyers told him not to. "Who does he think he is?" was their attitude. In his 1982, book *Mega Trends*, John Naisbitt describes lawyers as "beavers who damn up the stream and then only let water pass as they decide appropriate." All metaphors have limitations but this was pretty much our case. Our lawyers didn't have any reason not to proceed, they had no substantive objections, they simply said, "We are the lawyers and we are telling you to stop." So our general said no, move forward and if they present anything substantive we will stop and listen.

Having changed organizations, I am now working for a different brigadier general. I briefed him after my meeting with the DoDIG. He spoke with a number of people involved in my project and then told me he had confirmed everything I reported and that I had nothing to worry about. He cautioned me not to contact the SES or the general directly because I could trust them to validate the accuracy of my story. Additionally, to an investigator it might appear to be an attempt to synchronize our stories.

A week after of my meeting with the DoD IG, I found myself in the newspapers and the investigation being discussed on CSPAN. Many major newspapers reported that the Army had launched a criminal investigation into my settlement. "What on earth is this about?" my wife asked me. The news stories asserted that I was the trigger man in a conspiracy to defraud the government out of maybe $60 million. When the newspapers, including the *Army Times*, called my home I chose not to speak with any of them. I had felt some stress at different times in my career but nothing like this, being fired was one thing but going to jail was totally different. On a happy note, one of the articles in the *Phoenix Gazette* reported that I had been promoted to lieutenant colonel.

I met again with my new general and he said, "You have cooperated enough. You have been forthcoming and everyone involved tells me you are being truthful and I've also been assured that you have nothing to worry about. But there are forces at work that I don't understand and I think it's time for you to have a defense attorney. Someone who is only looking out for your best interest." I was both puzzled by this but somehow I was also happy because I was feeling very much alone and now I would have someone helping me. I responded, "Yes, sir, I think you are right. But I didn't understand my situation at all. Why doesn't the first general simply make a clear statement of the facts just as I have and put an end to this?"

My general told me, "As a general officer he has to handle this slowly and deliberately. He has to let this work it's course but you are in no danger. Keep your head down and let this burn itself out. Meanwhile I will tell our legal department that you are not talking to anyone until you have an Army Defense Attorney."

The situation had been elevated but I was glad to hear him speak like this. It was actually funny a week later when one of our in-house Army lawyers asked to meet with me and then presented himself as my defense attorney. "If I'm court martialed, are you the one who will represent me at trial?" I asked.

"Well no," he said sheepishly, "I can only give you advise about contracting."

"Thanks for your interest in my situation but I think my time is better spent talking with a defense attorney," I told him graciously.

So I'm on my own. How do I find a defense attorney? The only Army lawyer I knew was a friend I made at the Command and General Staff College and happily I found that he was stationed only four hours away. I called and arranged to meet him for lunch and after listening to my story he connected me with an excellent defense attorney from the Regional Office of the Army's Judge Advocate General Corps. I was fortunate that he accepted my case and held my hand for the next three years. I don't know what became of him but I hope he became the Judge Advocate General for the Army.

It's hard to compress three years of interrogations into anything interesting but I will give you my best summary. Over a period of three years, I was interrogated by agents of the Army Criminal Investigation Division (CID), interviewed by representatives from a number of higher headquarters and ultimately gave depositions to attorneys at the Armed Services Board of Contract Appels (ASBCA). Overall, I learned that once the government goes public with an investigation, they never admit they are wrong and close it. Instead of closing it, they simply change the allegation and start fishing in another spot hoping to hit on something. I presume my investigation is still open somewhere.

My investigation had four distinct phases. The Phase One Allegation was that I had conspired to defraud the government out of $60 million dollars by settling the audits without legal concurrence. The result of this phase was that the criminal investigators were totally confused by the Federal Acquisition Regulation (FAR) but in the end could find no evidence to support the allegation of conspiracy to defraud. When Phase One produced nothing, the government changed the allegation and went to Phase Two.

The Phase Two allegation was that although I may not be a crook, I was clearly an incompetent contracting officer. During this phase our higher headquarters sent a team and audited our entire contracting organization. Since the allegation was now about the technical aspects of contracting it made sense that they would do this. But frankly I'm being generous with them because what it really was is that they could smell blood in the water and wanted to get on the kill. With their audit completed, they reported that they found errors in 50 percent of the contracts they audited. But specific to my project, they found it be absolutely 100 percent perfect work. They could find no errors and they reported that it was actually "commendable contract work." I breathed a sigh of relief.

Now apparently cleared of being a crook and of being incompetent, I thought the government would drop the investigation. So I was very much surprised when the investigators went to Phase Three and told me that I was being investigated for committing adultery with employees of the helicopter company. I asked the investigator "with whom have I done this?" The investigator responded with a raised eyebrow and "you know who and you're going to tell me." At this point, I gave up cooperating and left the room. Of course there was no adultery so this phase also went nowhere.

So after over two years and finding nothing to charge me with, the Army went to Phase Four and assigned a "Disinterested Colonel" to perform an AR15-6 Investigation. The essence of an AR15-6 investigation is simply for the investigator to state if he believes something was done wrong. There is no threshold that has to be reached to determine that a crime has been committed. I have seen many of these investigations and frequently the investigator simply reports what his boss wants him to report. Without talking to me, the investigating colonel reviewed the written record and reported that something was done wrong and that I should be held responsible and punished. Exactly what was done wrong or exactly what I should be held responsible for was not presented in the report. It was merely a subjective assessment of "where there's smoke there must be fire."

About this time, Washington reassigned me to another location on the far side of the country. I wanted to stay where I was and retire and was initially resentful that I was moved. After some time went by it occurred to me that maybe my current general thought it best to remove me from a very uncomfortable environment and put me somewhere that I could breath. If that was his motivation, I owe that general a note of gratitude. The investigation was still hanging over me but it was a quiet year and I didn't have people ducking into rooms or crossing the street when they saw me. Absent any criminal prosecution, this Audit Closure Project had moved through contracting channels and was now before the Armed

Services Board of Contract Appeals (ASBCA). I was summoned to Washington, DC, to be "deposed" by lawyers representing both sides. "Deposed" means that you are questioned under oath with a court recorder taking dictation and if you are found to be lying you will be charged with perjury.

During this deposition process, it was also revealed to me that for the previous three years of interviews both the SES and the initial general officer had repeatedly denied they had given directions or had even been involved with closing these audits. Beyond that, they both gave very poor opinions of me personally and had used terms such as "an unreliable and marginal officer." Now it was clear to me why this ordeal had drug on for so long. Why would anyone believe me when two general officers were saying I was lying?

One of the good things about the deposition process is that everyone including the generals are put under oath for the first time. I had always been under oath but my accusers had not. When he was placed under oath my SES could not explain what his instructions to me to "execute" the settlement of the audits meant. But the highlight of this deposition phase was when the OER recording my work on this project was read into the court record. Faced with the statements he had written in my OER "singularly exceptional performance closing thirty-five audits, abilities exceed those of the most experienced civilian contracting officers, etc.," the general decided to back away from their previous denials and derogatory statements. I'm sure the general was thinking, "Why in the hell did I insist on writing that." But I was thinking, "I didn't want it but thank you God for putting that in place."

For the general it was exactly like the trial scene from the fictional movie "The Caine Mutiny." In that scene Captain Queeg (Humphrey Bogart) testifies that his executive officer, Lt. Maryk is a "disloyal and cowardly officer" and he is then required to read the efficiency report he wrote describing Lt. Maryk as "consistently loyal, courageous, and efficient, etc." Obviously he was unable to reconcile the discrepancy between his testimony and his written record.

The general was not alone. It played out that all the people who had been my most vocal critics, especially the contracting lawyers, once they were put under oath, would no longer defend the strong accusations they had leveled against me when they had anonymity. Being under oath and facing perjury charges turns out to be a very good mechanism for getting to the truth. After the last ASBCA deposition the whole investigation lost steam. What came out of the ASBCA was my total vindication from the criminal accusations, total validation of my work and the validation of my character.

Did I feel betrayed? Absolutely, I did. The moment you realize that you have been betrayed is perhaps the most painful you will experience. I view the betrayal by the SES and the general differently. The SES was only a civilian and they are frequently simply political appointees with no formal leadership or ethics development. But the general was a general and the ethos of "duty, honor, county" and "I will not lie, cheat, or steal or tolerate anyone who does" are absolutely required of him. I had carried the weight of this investigation for three years waiting for the general to speak up and now I knew the reason why he hadn't. He wasn't simply being silent, he had become one of my accusers. But why would a general lie over a simple contracting matter? The best I can do with my limited vocabulary is to say that he is a pathetic coward and weasel. C. S. Lewis might say something like "he is human vermin."

By this time, a totally different general was sitting in judgment over the investigation and he decided to take action by giving me a "Letter of Admonishment." The basis of the admonishment was not that I had done anything wrong, but that I had been the focal point of an embarrassing situation for the Army. Although I wasn't happy about being punished in any manner, at least I wasn't going to jail over this.

I must gratefully acknowledge that my GS-15 stuck with me through all of this. It probably cost him his own opportunity for promotion to SES but he was unflinching in telling the truth and supporting me. I will be forever grateful to him.

Was this general the worse leader I would fall victim to? Yes, he at least ties for the worse. In my earlier "If They Can't Fly I Want Their Wings" adventure, I told you about a battalion commander who carelessly put pilots in danger of death. I said that in the Army this is the great sin and absolutely the worse thing a commander can do. But now I had a general who was willing to let me go to prison for following his totally legitimate orders. So he at least ties for the worse.

To summarize the lessons from this "You Need A Defense Attorney" adventure. First, you must do the right thing every time. My "60 Minutes Test" that I developed and promoted early in my career was now very much a reality as I was tasked to explain why all my actions over a broad spectrum of accusations had each been correct. If I had been found lacking in any of the areas investigated I would have been cashiered out of the Army and probably put in prison.

Second, Soldiers must have trust and confidence in the orders their leaders give them. It is the glue that holds the military system together. When a general orders you onto a hostile beach you can't be worried that he will abandon you there when the political winds change. In this case my trust was terribly misplaced and it was my long pattern of pursuing the right thing that saved me when this general abandoned me on this beach.

Third, I spent twenty years in the company of brave men. Beyond the physical danger of combat, what these men feared most is that at some point, their courage might fail them and they would betray their friends. This failure can happen to the most junior officers or even a general officer.

Fourth, I didn't tell my children this story until they were adults. We all use this experience to keep our problems in perspective and will frequently remark, "I don't like it but at least no one is trying to put me in prison."

CHAPTER 12

Humor Can Be Dangerous

This is another chapter I didn't want to write. If you're not interested in what causes me to laugh, skip this chapter.

Humor is one of the great attributes of God and one of his great gifts to us. Humor is what allows me to look at a lousy situation and remark, "I don't like it but at least no one is trying to put me in jail." But there is no value at generating humor at some else's expense or when it's simply meant to be hurtful to them. Certainly bullies think they are being funny and their friends all yuck it up but secretly they are all waiting their turn to become the target. Bullies, like bad leaders, are monotonously similar.

When my youngest daughter was in high school she met a new boy who asked, "What does your father do?"

"He's a retired Army Officer," she told him. Much to her surprise, he responded, "That must be awful, is he terribly stern?"

"No he's really funny and a lot of fun," she told him. I understand that the boy had a valid perception that military people can be humorless and unapproachable and certainly some are but not me and not my friends.

My family finds humor in the cycle we call the "law of natural consequence," which is simply a warning—followed by noncompliance, resulting in a consequence. When my girls were very young we had a memorable weekend camping trip that we still talk about thirty years later. When we talk about it now, they don't remember the swimming or hiking, they remember three events. First, "Dad told Kelli not to play on the rocks next to the water because they were covered with moss and she would slip into the lake—end result was Kelli didn't comply and slipped into the lake." Second, "Then Dad told Kelli not to play on the cable fencing because she would fall off and get hurt—end result was Kelli didn't comply and fell off the cable and hurt her leg." Third, "Then Dad told Kelli not to play on the big concrete mound because she would fall and get hurt—end result was Kelli slipped and rolled down the mound skinning her legs." What we see humor in was this cycle of father's warning, noncompliance and predicted consequence.

We have another adventure where my competence was not as predicative. When the girls were grades 5, 8, 11, we moved to New Hampshire. The night of the first good snowstorm I said, "It's such a great snowy night, let's go to Dunkin' Donuts and get a snack and watch the snow fall!"

"No," my wife said, "there is no point going out and getting in an accident."

"Don't be foolish, I grew up driving in the snow, you can stay home but we are going," I told her. So I took the girls and we headed down the hill in our front wheel drive Dodge minivan. "Girls, it's important to check how slippery the road is so watch this as I touch the brakes and test for traction," I told them. "Oh, oh, hang on" was the next thing I said, as the car's back end slid around and headed down the hill backward. Bang, we went backward into the snowbank, which spun us back around and we were now going hood first and I eased to a stop. The kiss with the snowbank broke the seal on one of the back tires so now I had to change a flat tire.

"Maybe we should go home," the girls offered. But I was a man on a mission and said, "No, I'm not going home without a doughnut." At Dunkin' Donuts, I conducted a "post-accident briefing" and discussed how we had all learned that front wheel drive minivans handle differently than rear wheel cars on snow. I also told them not to tell their mother about all the fun we had. When we got home my wife asked what had taken so long so I told her I had a flat tire. "How on earth did that happen?" she asked. The girls respectfully remained silent so I came clean and told her the whole story. We still laugh about how there can be a cycle of a mother's warning, fathers noncompliance, and predicted consequence.

Sometime humor can be a gift to strangers. I have a wonderful family photo from the night the 1984 Los Angeles Olympics closed. The picture wasn't taken in Los Angeles; it was taken in the Airport at Dothan Alabama. At that time I was assigned at Ft. Rucker Al and the closest commercial airport was at Dothan about twenty miles away. This was a very small regional airport serviced by only one major airline and one of the smaller air carriers with maybe a total of six inbound flights each day. The night of the Olympic Closing Ceremony my wife was scheduled to land in Dothan after being gone on a business trip. Our daughters were two, four, and six and our normal procedure was that the girls would put on good dresses and we would take flowers to welcome her home at the airport.

That evening, I had the girls dressed and watching TV in the living room while I finished doing the dishes and watching the Olympics in the kitchen. I realized that the closing ceremony was going to take place at the exact time my wife was landing. Then it hit me like a diamond bullet right in the brain. I told the girls that we were going to do something special this time. I told them that they would wear their gymnastics outfits and that we would make a sign out of poster board and they could decorate it. So after a flurry of activity the girls had changed into gymnastics outfits and we had a sign with a lot of nice artwork and it said, "Welcome Home, Mom, US Olympic Swim Team."

When we got to the airport it was packed with about fifty people. "What's going on?" I thought. "The plane only holds twelve people." Then I saw that they had one of those long banner type signs that you make on your home computer. "Um," I thought, "I wonder who Don Brown is and where he's been?" Just as we walked in there was an announcement that the plane was on final and would touch down in three minutes. This was the small regional airline, which only held about twelve passengers, and I knew that the passengers would get off the plane and walk into the terminal through the counter space down the hallway so I took the girls and propped them up with the sign on a couple of chairs across from ticket counter. I chuckled to myself because the big group was in the lobby, which was the wrong place. I was in the right place. Almost immediately, the plane taxied up and the passengers started getting off. The group realized their mistake and came running to stand in front of us to welcome Don Brown.

One of the ladies was struggling to get their banner up and looked at us and said, "Look they have a sign also." Then she shouted with excitement, "Oh my God, there's someone from the Olympics on the plane!" It was like someone had shouted "fire" as everyone was saying something about the Olympics.

"Did you talk to the Olympic swimmer?" someone asked the first passenger to reach the counter.

"What are you talking about?" he asked.

"You idiot, there's an Olympic swimmer on your plane, that's her family over there with the sign, and the flowers, and the coordinated gymnastics outfits," he was told. As everyone looked at us, I told the girls to shout "welcome home, Mommy" as loud as they could and to wave. It was pandemonium and when my wife could see us and wave, people started clapping and saying things to her like "good job and welcome home." In the next instant, she was hugging the girls and asked me "What's going on?"

"Read the sign," I said.

"You're an idiot!" she told me in a whisper. "Smile and go with it, these people want to be part of your adventure," I told her. Poor Don Brown, it was simply his bad luck to get on a plane with an Olympic swimmer. As we waited for our bags, people where respectful and gave us our privacy as they kind of made a big circle around us listening to everything we said and chatting with excitement. I could tell some people were skeptical, but they still hung on wanting to be part of the adventure. Someone asked about the *Dothan Newspaper*, which created a buzz and gave me the opportunity to ask someone to take our picture. Camera flash and newspaper talk added fuel to the fire. Fortunately, with a small operation like Dothan, it only takes a few minutes for the bags to come out. Then we were in the car and my wife scolded me asking, "What did you think you were doing?"

"Hell, I thought we would be the only people there, who knew half the town would be there. But this was a gift to them, when they go to church tomorrow they are going to tell everyone that they saw you, an Olympic swimmer at the airport. Besides you were the captain of the girls swim team in high school so if you hadn't married me, who knows what you could have accomplished."

"You're just an idiot" she said. Although this joke spun out of control, I don't think it hurt anyone. I have convinced myself that it was a gift to all those people.

Sometimes humor can make you humble. Easter Sunrise Service at Ft. Rucker is held at the swimming beach. The geographic layout has three parts. The Command Group Party has seats on the dock. There are bleachers at the water's edge for families with little kids who need to be seated. There is a twenty-foot high bank a little off the water where about one thousand people can stand and look down at the service. Standing on the bank is preferred because you can move around, you look down on everyone, and you can be the first out of the parking lot when it's over. So I'm sitting in the bleachers with wife and three daughters aged two, four, and six and we are all wearing our good Easter clothes, which includes hats for the girls. My two-year-old got restless and I'm trying to get her settled down and she decides that I should wear her hat. So of course to keep her quite I let her put her hat on my head. Once she has the hat on my head, she considers it and decides to put it back on her head and to my relief remain quite. On Monday, my phone was ringing off the hook with people telling me "nice hat Cobra Pilot, we were all on the bank watching your daughter and we knew that you were going to wear the hat to keep her quite, well done, and you looked good." My daughters don't remember that but it is part of our family comical history.

Sometimes humor can expedite things. Again back in the 1980s, one of my sisters had just delivered a baby back home, so I called the hospital to talk with her. Back then, long-distance telephone calls were expensive and I didn't want to be put on hold by the hospital operator. So I called from the comfort of my kitchen at Ft. Rucker and I shouted into the phone, "This is Captain Hancock calling from Nicaragua and I would like to speak with my sister Michele but I don't know what room she is in."

"Stop yelling," said the operator. "I'm having trouble hearing you, there are helicopters running outside my window, can you hear me?" I asked her.

"I hear you fine, just stop yelling and I will get Michele," the operator then quickly found my sister. That night my mother called me to report that her friend Maryann had called asking about me being in Nicaragua. I was truthful and told my mother it was a small lie to avoid being put on hold and running up my phone bill. "Just tell Maryann that I'm not allowed to discuss it," I told her. So in a small way, I brightened the day for a number of my mother's friends as they reflected on me performing important military duties in Nicaragua.

There are situations where humor can be dangerous. Clearly the malicious humor imposed by bullying is simply mean and bad. But you can hurt someone's feeling with no intention of doing so. Sometimes I'm in a meeting or social sitting and something will come up that makes me want to bust out with a clever response that I'm sure is absolutely hilarious but I have learned to stop and ask myself "is this going to be funny to everyone, is there something I don't understand or not aware of and can this be hurtful to someone?" So I try to contain myself and think before I blurt out what I'm thinking. The subjects we talk about and the language we use can be acceptable or offensive based on the social setting we are in. For example, I am always quick to admit that when it comes to music, "I am musically retarded. I have no ability to hit a note or carry a tune." I freely make this evaluation about myself. I think it is absolutely clear and accurate so I think it's fine. But not so fast, Mr. Tin-ear, the word *retarded* is absolutely prohibited in some social circles so instead of receiving sympathy for my musical ineptitude, I am attacked for being a vulgar, insensitive, and mean old man. So what is acceptable in the hockey locker room may not be acceptable at the PTA meeting. When I make these mistakes with my family, they correct me gently by telling me "humor can be dangerous."

ENDING

Have I Been Effective?

When I meet God, one of my first questions will be, "Why did You allow me to stay in the Army for twenty years?"

In chapter 1, I said the purpose of telling my stories was my hope that they would be an encouragement to anyone who faces similar problems in their jobs and to reassure you that God is watching over you and has a plan for you. You do the right thing every time and let God handle the fall out. I hope that I have been effective in doing this. As a bonus, it would be nice if you found my stories entertaining in some way.

In chapter 1, I said that writing in a conversational style means that I have to place material in a sequence that is new to me. That is the case now. In my original draft, I had the some of the following material at the front because that's how I think it should go. But now you see I have it at the very end.

Before I can close my book, I have to be absolutely clear that the Army was good to me and for me. Only in America can you run away from home, join the Army and get to do the things I've done simply because you have the ability and are willing to go do them. No other country in the world provides opportunities like this.

For most of my career, the Army slogan was "Be All You Can Be." I can't think of a more personally empowering slogan. It clearly and simply tells you, "Look, the opportunities are here, it is up to you to apply yourself and reach for them." The flip side of course is that you are responsible to reach for the opportunities and if you don't, it's your own fault. The lyrics of this old song capture this idea.

> *"I met a man who had a dream he had since he was 20, I met that man when he was 81, He said too many folks just stand and wait until the morning, Don't they know tomorrow never comes?"*
> *(Roger Wittaker,*
> *New World in the Morning)*

My stories focused on bad situations with bad leaders. This was necessary because the point of the book is to present difficult situations that made me question why I was in the Army. But embedded in those stories you can see that at the critically right times God brought me good, no He brought me super leaders. These leaders gave me the perspective that I brought value to the Army, had contributions to make and taught me important lessons that made me better in all aspects. Below are three examples of super leaders and lessons they taught me.

In chapter 3, "Professionalism: Money," embedded in that story I told you about a Super Infantry Battalion commander that I served under when I was lieutenant in Germany. At his departing dinner, he was asked how he was able to handle the pressures of being a battalion commander on the Russian Front (old Cold War slang). His answer went like this, "No matter what pressure I'm feeling, I know that when I look in the mirror I have to answer three questions: am I a good Christian, am I a good husband and father, and am I a good soldier. If I ensure these priorities guide my decisions, I can face any negative fallout that might come my way." When he said this, it was absolutely clear, it was like a diamond bullet to the brain, this is what we had observed and admired in him for the two years he commanded us. At that time, I was not a Christian but I knew that this was how I had to approach my life. He is one of the four finest men I have ever known.

In chapter 8, "If They Can't Fly I Want Their Wings," embedded in that story I told you about a Super Aviation Battalion commander that I served under when I was a captain. The Battalion had five companies and each company had a different organizational structure, different mission and different equipment. The commander was wrapping up one of our weekly command and staff meetings and he kept the company commanders behind and said this, "You men are not competing against each other. You each have different companies with different issues and each day brings you different problems to solve. I will not evaluate you by measuring you against each other, I will evaluate each of you on what you do with your companies and how you handle the problems you face." I saw the wisdom in this and from that point forward I made certain that I communicated this same message to my own subordinate officers. He is also one of the four finest men I have ever known.

In chapter 9, "Just Sign the Inventory," embedded in that story I told you about an Assistant Division commander (brigadier general) in an Infantry Division when I was a captain trusted with command of an Aviation Company. He was a speaker at the Division's In-house Company Commander's Pre-Command Course. His advice went like this: "As a commander you will be juggling many things and will sometime feel you are under pressure, you will face a problem and think, 'If I just take a shortcut, this problem will go away and I can move to the next problem.' When that happens you need to stop, you need to remember that there are no shortcuts, shortcuts will lead to bigger problems downstream. Do the right thing every time, regardless of the immediate negative consequences." This was important advice and it served me very well as a company commander. It continues to serve me well these many years later and it always will.

Life in the military is largely about relationships. I think the relationship between British Army Lts. C. S. Lewis and Edward "Paddy" Moore epitomizes the best relationship between two Soldiers. Lewis and Moore served together as Infantry lieutenants in WWI and had a pact that if either died during the war, the survivor would take care of the others family. Moore was killed in France and Lewis was wounded. After recovering from his wounds, Lewis fulfilled his commitment and took care of Moore's family. When I was an Infantry lieutenant, first in Korea and then in Germany, I would ask myself, "If this blows up and I'm killed in the first artillery barrage of the first battle, who do I trust to take care of my family and help them manage my finances?" I spent much of my career seeking this type of close relationship and was fortunate to find at least two. When you find that relationship it's magical.

In closing this book, it's fair for me to answer the question, "Why do I think God allowed me to stay in the Army for twenty years?" Please remember that I'm only a "C student" and not intuitive so this is my best explanation.

"For I know the plans I have for you..." (Jeremiah 29:11)

God has a plan for each of us. But how do you know what that plan is? How do you know you are where God wants you to be? God normally shapes our circumstances by opening and closing doors. Sometimes we balk at these opportunities because we misunderstand them, are afraid of extending ourselves, or simply don't want to do it. As you see from my stories, I had trouble seeing God's hand in much of what I was experiencing. In the end, I think the reasons were as follows:

Overall, it would have broken my heart if I had failed to complete the twenty-year career. All I ever wanted to be was a soldier, to wear the uniform, shoulder responsibilities, lead troops, do exciting things, and to have people look at me and expect that I will act as a gentleman, with courage and with honor. I was fortunate that circumstances placed me in a small state college that had ROTC so that I became an officer. If I had failed making it to twenty years, it would have shaken my self-identity and self-worth. I think this was a gift but only secondary to the things that follow.

First, I was to present a model of faith and good conduct to my family. During my time in the Army, I had several opportunities where I could express to my wife and children that our family unit and each of them individually was more important to me than my Army career. I tried to include them in selecting where my (our) next assignment would be. These choices decided whether we would be together or separated and the location where they would live. As my children grew older I could select times where it was appropriate to discuss a specific problem I had faced and how it applied to something they were facing. The message I needed to convey was that we will face problems but we always do what we know is the right thing. God is interested in each of us personally and we need to let God work out the future.

Second, I was to present a Godly response to the people who I had conflict with. Our purpose on earth is to glorify God and that includes the things we do, the things we don't do and also how we conduct ourselves through all of it. When we deal with difficult people or have conflict we need to respond with a quiet confidence that doing what we know is right will always provide the best result, the greatest contentment, and ultimately the greatest reward. This doesn't mean I don't get angry or that my feelings don't get hurt. There are times when I have to stand at attention and take it on the chin and I absolutely hate it when this happens. I know that I act much better when I can step back and get my anger or frustration under control before I have to speak or act. I act infinitely much better when I pray about the problem first. My biggest mistakes and my biggest regrets all resulted from me acting when I was angry.

Third, it was to prepare me for responsibilities I have after the Army. After the Army, I ended up starting and running a small business and for reasons that are simply a mystery to me, God has chosen to bless me and the company has grown and prospered.

But specific to the purpose of this book, I will report a discussion that took place at a local college. My company business manager was enrolled in a master's in business administration program. It was a night program so most students were a few years out of college and working in an assortment of industries. During one of the classes the professor asked each student to summarize the insurance and other benefits that their companies provided. The result was that my company had the best benefits program. The professor offered that he was surprised that a small business could offer the best benefits program of all the companies represented. My manager's response was simply this: "The owner of my company is a retired Army Officer and he is intent on doing the best that he can for his employees." This approach largely represents the attitudes and values I developed through my experiences in the Army. As a student of business, I know that this violates Business 101, which tells us that the purpose of business is to maximize profit. My business model makes it difficult for me to compete in the market place and we often lose work when the customer selects the winner simply based on the lowest price. But it works well enough and I'm content that when I do win, it has nothing to do with me. When I win it's because God wants me here and the people I employ need these jobs.

Last spring, I was back in my home town to meet with the owners of a small business who wanted to discuss how we could team and pursue different projects together. One of the owners asked me two questions that I think round out this book. The first question was "what is the key to your business success?" I told her "my business has grown and prospered but it is a mystery to me why God has chosen for this to happen. I will ask Him when I see Him. But I had the good fortune when I was young, to have a commander tell me that being a Christian, husband/father and soldier in that order, was the foundation of living up to the expectations of Army service. This foundation has also been an essential part of bringing useful lessons from the Army to my work afterward." The second question was "When did you realize that you needed to leave here to seek a career?" "It was sixth grade when I had to wear my sister's pants to school," was my immediate response.

ABOUT THE AUTHOR

Rick Hancock is a nondenominational Protestant. He is a retired Army Officer and currently the owner of Hancock Management LLC, a small management consulting company. Rick entered the Army through the Army ROTC program and served twenty years active duty. He is both a paratrooper and helicopter pilot and served in both Infantry and Aviation Units. His education is a bachelor's degree from Lake Superior State College and a master's degree from the University of Southern California. His published writings include a number of technical articles on Army helicopter tactics and management.